D1256315

A PEEP INTO THE PAST
and other prose pieces

BOOKS BY MAX BEERBOHM

Essays, criticism, short stories and other prose pieces
The Works of Max Beerbohm
More
Yet Again
And Even Now
A Variety of Things
Mainly on the Air
Around Theatres
More Theatres
Last Theatres
The Incomparable Max *selected and introduced by* SIR SYDNEY *Roberts*
A Peep into the Past and Other Prose Pieces *collected and introduced
    by Rupert Hart-Davis*

Verse
Max in Verse: Rhymes and Parodies *collected and annotated* by J. G. Riewald

Stories, character sketches
The Happy Hypocrite
A Christmas Garland (*parodies*)
Seven Men (*reissued 1950 as* Seven Men and Two Others)
The Dreadful Dragon of Hay Hill

Novel
Zuleika Dobson

Caricatures, cartoons
Caricatures of Twenty-five Gentlemen
The Poets' Corner
A Book of Caricatures
The Second Childhood of John Bull
Fifty Caricatures
A Survey
Rossetti and his Circle
Things New and Old
Observations

A PEEP
INTO THE PAST

and other prose pieces

by
MAX BEERBOHM

collected and introduced by
RUPERT HART-DAVIS

THE STEPHEN GREENE PRESS
BRATTLEBORO, VERMONT

First American Edition 1972

This book has been produced in Great Britain

It is published by the Stephen Greene Press,
Brattleboro, Vermont 05301.

Library of Congress Catalog Card Number: 72-79560
International Standard Book Number: 0-8289-0169-4

Contents

Words for Pictures

Introduction

Oscar Wilde said that the gods had bestowed on Max the gift of perpetual old age, and now, on his hundredth birthday, we can discern more clearly than ever the profound truth of that remark. For, like his lifelong friend Will Rothenstein, Max stepped very early on to the public scene, fully armed with pen and pencil, and though he later refined and perfected his use of both, he immediately adopted the mould and the mask that he was never to relinquish. The pieces collected in this volume cover more than half a century, but the same voice is instantly recognised in all of them. I have arranged them chronologically, so that the reader may see how, while Max as it were stood still, society and the world about him moved relentlessly on.

His forty Italian years were mostly spent drawing and enjoying the sunshine, but before his marriage and migration in 1910 he had for some fifteen years earned his living as an unexpectedly industrious journalist. Besides his weekly theatre article for the *Saturday Review*, he contributed essays on a multitude of subjects and non-subjects to a surprising variety of newspapers and periodicals. From them he assembled the material for his books of essays: *The Works of Max Beerbohm* (1896), *More* (1899), *Yet Again* (1909), *And Even Now* (1920). Despite the intrusion of *Mainly on the Air* (1946), I was tempted to continue the sequence, and only unwillingness to vex the shade of the great Ruskin prevented my titling this volume *Unto This Last*.

Thanks to the researches of Dr J. G. Riewald, the late Allan Wade and others, I was able to choose from almost ninety pieces—enough for three books of this size. Most of them were finished essays, but some were book-reviews, obituary tributes and other occasional writings. Presumably Max considered and rejected most of them as unworthy of resurrection, but I like to think that some he may simply have forgotten. Else how could he leave unreprinted the perceptive analysis of Oscar Wilde in "A Lord of Language," the sharply clear pen-portrait of Andrew Lang? In any case authors are seldom the best judges of their own writings, and posterity is ruthless in separating the gold from the dross.

All the uncollected pieces have flashes of the true Max in them, but he was right to reject the majority. Many are too topical for permanence, some deal with themes and persons about whom Max later wrote more fully, others were simply space-fillers. I have chosen only those items which, in my opinion, will enhance rather than detract from Max's reputation. None of them has appeared in a book by Max, except for the introduction to his collected edition, which is now an expensive and almost unprocurable luxury.

Referring to A. B. Walkley, Max used words that apply perfectly to himself: "Collection is a great test. Things that seem good enough separately may be tedious in a gathering of them. But really good things help one another loyally. . . . Very light they seem. But the secret of that effect is in the perfection of the workmanship."

Except for the three extracts from Max's manuscripts, every text is taken from the book or periodical in which it appeared. I have corrected a few spelling slips and printers' errors, and have unified such details as the italicisation of book-titles and foreign words. A few passages cry out for annotation, but I cannot imagine Max approving, so I have sternly restricted the footnotes to details of original printings.

My grateful thanks go to Max's sister-in-law Mrs Eva Reichmann for her trust and forbearance over many years; to the Editor of *The Times* for permission to reprint two pieces; and to Mr Simon Nowell-Smith for much expert help and guidance.

Max once said that he reckoned there were fifteen hundred people in this country, and maybe a thousand in America, who knew what he was at. It is to them, with homage to a writer and caricaturist of genius, that I offer this centenary tribute.

RUPERT HART-DAVIS

Marske-in-Swaledale
April 1972

A PEEP INTO THE PAST
AND OTHER PROSE PIECES

A Peep into the Past[1]

SCAR WILDE! I wonder to how many of my readers the jingle of this name suggests anything at all? Yet, at one time, it was familiar to many and if we search back among the old volumes of Mr Punch, we shall find many a quip and crank cut at its owner's expense. But time is a quick mover and many of us are fated to outlive our reputations and thus, though at one time Mr Wilde, the old gentleman, of whom we are going to give our readers a brief account, was in his way quite a celebrity; today his star is set, his fame obscured in this busy changeful city.

Once a welcome guest in many of our Bohemian haunts, he lives now a life of quiet retirement in his little house in Tite Street with his wife and his two sons, his prop and mainstay, solacing himself with many a reminiscence of the friends of his youth, whilst he leaves his better known brother, William, to perpetuate the social name of the family. Always noted for his tenacious memory, it is one of the old gentleman's keenest pleasures to regale a visitor from the outer world with stories of the late Mr Frank Miles, Mr Godwin, the architect, Mr Robert Browning or the Earl of

---

[1] Written in December 1893 or very early in 1894, when Max was an undergraduate of twenty-one, and Oscar Wilde, at the height of his success, was thirty-nine. On the manuscript, beneath the title, Max wrote: "For the 1st No. of the *Yellow Book*" (though he later forgot this, and denied that the essay was so intended). When the first number appeared in April 1894 Max's contribution was "A Defence of Cosmetics." A year later Wilde's downfall made "A Peep into the Past" unpublishable, and its only appearance has been in an unauthorised edition of 300 copies, published in New York in 1923. The original manuscript is in the Berg Collection in the New York Public Library, where the text has been kindly checked for me by Mr Frank Mattson.

Lytton, who was not the only member of the upper ten thousand to honour Mr Wilde with his personal friendship. "All, all are gone, the old familiar faces" and with the quiet resignation of one who knows that he is the survivor of a bygone day, Mr Wilde tends more and more to exist in its memory or to solace himself with the old classics of which he was ever so earnest a student, with his Keats and his Shakespeare, his Joseph Miller and the literal translations of the Greek Dramatists. Not that he is a mere *laudator temporis acti*, a bibliophile and nothing more. He still keeps up his writing, is still the glutton for work that he always was. He has not yet abandoned his old intention of dramatising Salome, and the amount of journalistic matter that he quietly produces and contributes anonymously to various periodicals is surprising. Only last year an undergraduate journal called the *Spirit Lamp* accepted a poem of his in which there were evidences that he has lost little of his old talent for versification.

Mr Wilde is an early riser. Every morning, winter and summer at 4.30 a.m. his portly form—(he is in appearance not unlike Sir William Harcourt and still stands six foot three in his slippers)—may be seen bending over the little spirit-kettle, at which he boils himself his cup of hot cocoa. Donning his work-a-day clothes, he proceeds at once to his study and commences work, continuing steadily till breakfast, which he takes in company with his wife and sons. Himself most regular in his habits, he is something of a martinet about punctuality in his household and perhaps this accounts for the constant succession of page-boys, which so startles the neighbourhood. Breakfast over, the master of the house enjoys his modest cigarette—no costly cigar or precious meerschaum ever passes his lips—he is a strict believer in simplicity of life as the hand-maiden of hard work. He never nowadays even looks at the morning papers, so wholly has he cut himself off from society, though he still goes on taking in the *Athenaeum*, in the hopes that it may even now do the same to him. So without dawdling over the perusal of news, he immediately resumes work and does not desist until the stroke of twelve, when punctually he folds up his papers, wipes his pen, puts away his books of reference and starts for an hour's walk up and down the King's Road, Chelsea. With his tall bowed figure, carefully brushed silk hat and frock coat, which though old-fashioned was evidently cut by a good tailor, old Mr Wilde is well-known to all frequenters of the thoroughfare. The tradespeople, too, know him well and often waylay him as he attempts to pass on.

After early dinner, the time is passed pleasantly in reading Ruskin to his two youngsters; after that more literary work, a light supper, a glass of grog and bed-time. But not always rest! Often, his good lady tells me, has she woken at three or four in the morning to find her husband still sitting up in bed or pacing up and down the bedroom in parturition of that same joke of which he sketched for her the outline as they were retiring to rest. Yes, and it is in this indomitable perseverance, this infinite capacity for taking pains, this "grit," as they call it in the North, that lies Mr Wilde's secret. True that the whole body of his signed work is very small—a book of parodies upon Rossetti, a few fairy-tales in the manner of Hans Andersen, an experimental novel in the style of Poe, a volume of essays, which Mr Pater is often obliged blushingly to repudiate, a French play written in collaboration with M. Louÿs and one or two English ones in collaboration with Mr G. R. Sims. But surely we must judge an artist, not so much by his achievement as by his method of procedure, and though such a story as the *The Theory of Mr W. S.* (I came across a copy of it lately at an old bookstall in Vigo Street) occupied only the extreme middle of no more than forty pages, the author has given me his word that it took him six months' hard unremitting labour to complete.

After all, it is not so much as a literary man that Posterity will forget Mr Wilde, as in his old capacity of journalist. The visit to America, that is still so fresh in the old gentleman's memory, doubtless influenced his style in no small degree, and many an old pressman can testify to the great vivacity and humour of their colleague, though they may envy the indomitable vitality which enables one so far past his meridian to continue "producing." Perhaps the most startling feature of his career was the manner in which, putting his broad shoulder to the wheel, he was able so late in life to strike out into dramatic writing—a branch that he had never till then attempted. When Mr Sydney Cooper contributed to the last *Academy* but one a picture of a hunt scene, everyone was surprised, but that Oscar Wilde should have written a four-act play and got it produced by a London manager, fairly beat all records of senile enterprise. We critics were really touched and—who will blame us for it?—agreed to withhold those criticisms which we should otherwise have been forced to make upon the production. It was a pretty occasion and anyone who was present, as I was on the first night, will look back with affection at its memory. The play itself a chapter of reminiscences—the audience good natured and respectful—the hearty calls of "Author"—and finally his appearance before the curtain, bowing with old-fashioned grace to the Public whom he had served so faithfully. Those of us who had known him in the old days, observed that he seemed for the moment dazed and noted with feelings of pity that in his great excitement he had forgotten to extinguish his cigarette, an oversight that the Public was quick to pardon in the old gentleman.

Not long ago, wishing to verify one or two facts for an article I was writing upon the Wits of the Early Victorian Era and knowing that Mr Sala was out of town, I paid a visit to the little house in Tite Street. I found everything there neat and clean and, though, of course, very simple and unpretentious, bearing witness to womanly care and taste. As I was ushered into the little study, I fancied that I heard the quickly receding *frou-frou* of tweed trousers, but my

host I found reclining, hale and hearty, though a little
dishevelled, upon the sofa. With one hand readjusting the
nut-brown Georgian wig that he is accustomed to wear, he
motioned me with a courteous gesture of the other to an
arm-chair.

The old gentleman was unaffectedly pleased to receive a
visit from the outer world, for, though he is in most things
"a praiser of past times," yet he is always interested to hear
oral news of the present, and many young poets can testify
to the friendly interest in their future taken by a man who
is himself contented to figure in their past. As it was, when
I had enriched myself from the storehouse of his still un-
clouded memory, we fell to talking about things in general,
and I was struck by the quaint humour which still pervades
his talk as well as by the delightfully old-fashioned way in
which he rolls out his well-rounded periods. Many a modern
conversationist, I thought, might do worse than take a hint
or two from his style. Nor has he lost any of that old Irish
readiness for which he was once famed. It is said that at a
dinner given once at which many were present, Mr Whistler,
then quite a young boy, perpetrated some daring epigram
and Wilde, beaming kindly across the table, said, to encourage him, "How I wish I had said that!" Young impudence cried "You will, Sir, you will." "No, I won't,"
returned the elder man, quick as thought, and young impudence relapsed into silence abashed. Since then, the old
journalist has contracted a strange habit of chuckling to himself inordinately at whatever he says, and to such a degree
has this habit grown upon him that at the last dinner-party
he ever attended it was decided that he had the rare faculty
of keeping a whole table perfectly serious, whilst he himself
was convulsed with laughter. I think however it is only one
of the mannerisms of age, and certainly I found him as
amusing as ever he was and as prone to utter those bulls
which are an Irishman's privilege and are known in England
by the rather pretentious name of paradox. One instance will

[7]

suffice. After we had chatted together for a while, somebody entered to say that an old lady had called for the character of her new page-boy, and as my host with his passion for all literary work seemed anxious to write it, I felt I had better take my leave. Just as I was leaving the room I observed that the weather had become very sultry and I feared we should have a storm. "Ah yes," was the reply, "I expect we shall soon *see* the thunder and *hear* the lightning!" How delightful a perversion of words! I left the old gentleman chuckling immoderately at his little joke.

An Unhappy Poet

Bexhill-on-Sea is the haven for me
Whene'er my nerves are depressed;
For there's a retreat where you golf and you eat
And you sleep and you dream and you rest!

HESE EXQUISITE WORDS were written by one of the most prolific and, it may be, most popular of our modern poets, Mr Clement Scott. We quote them, not merely because their cadence has haunted us, and it is a pleasure to write them out, but also because they seem to epitomise the bitter tragedy of their writer's life.

Every great poet has had some one impulse, to which may be traced all that is finest in his work. It is a function of criticism to determine in each case what that impulse was. Some poets have been impelled by a love either of Liberty, or of Truth, or of Pleasure, or of their native land; others, again—and it may be that their work is the most enduring, τὸ ποιητικώτατον—by a love of Nature. Wordsworth loved Nature in all her manifestations; to him, sky, air, water, landscape, were all impressive and suggestive. Shelley was more particularly "the poet of the Clouds." Swinburne is the poet of the Sea. And Mr Clement Scott is the poet of the Seaside.

Circumstances, the curse of poets, compel this man to live in London, driving him in and out of glaring theatres, up and down Fleet Street. It is fearful to think of his soul being slowly crushed by so uncongenial a life. Many, many are the poems he has written about this or that seaside resort. Some of them, indeed, have evidently been written during a happy holiday, and are instinct with the joyous spirit of Saturday-to-Monday. But most, alas! have been wrung from him in smoky exile, and are suffused with melancholy, subdued, nostalgic. As in the lines written recently and quoted above, he writes most often, not with Horace's mild desire for the Sabine farm, but rather with Byron's terrible longing for Ravenna. Let our readers turn to his volume, *Lays and Lyrics*.

It was published eight years ago, but the spray is still salt upon its pages. When Scott (in the case of such a man we make no apology for dropping the Mr) sings the praises of this or that resort, he does it with an art so magical that we seem, ourselves, as we read, to be treading the jetty, or the sand, or the marine parade, as the case may be. Of Brighton he writes:

> *Wandering waves on the shingle dash,*
> *The sky's too blue for a thoughtless tear;*
> . . . .
> *Lazily lost in a dream we sit—*
> *Maidens' eyes are a waveless mere—*
> *There's many a vow when seagulls flit,*
> *And many a sigh when lamps are lit,*
> *And many a kiss upon Brighton Pier.*

And of Boulogne:

> *Old Albion's coast isn't lively, is it?*
> *There are jollier places, you'll all agree;*
> *So cross the Channel, and come to visit*
> *Our holiday life at Boulogne-on-Sea.*

Scott, you see, is not faithful to one love. What poet ever was? As the Pagan hymned Chloe, and Lydia, and Cynara, and Phyllis, so does Scott delight "to softly praise"—his own expression—places innumerable on our coast. He describes how he once found himself "on Margate pier, in a riotous round of women and wine;" and how "the Margate air was piercing sweet to the world and" him. His soft praises of Cromer are too well known to the admirers of Mr Isidore de Lara and the readers of the *Daily Telegraph* to need repetition. Indeed, though he has been enamoured often, he has never written so passionately as about "Poppyland." The Cornish coast is the only one of his loves that would seem to have left any bitterness in his bosom. We hold that the love tragedies of a poet are as sacred as those of any other man, but we must confess we are curious to know what prompted this poet to write so sombrely of

The rocks and the caves
Where the sea birds find their houses, and ignorant folks their
graves.

When he deals with more direct passions, with the love of a man for a woman, he is less happy perhaps. Now and again, however, the lady addressed seems to be rather an abstraction, a symbol for some seaside resort, and in these poems he is at his best. Take, for example, from the poem he calls "Violet" that stanza which runs thus:

You meet me with your beauty unimpaired—
I greet you with dull sorrow in my face;
You, with your haunting face, that souls ensnared—
I with a past no praying can retrace!
You can remember nothing—you are fair!
The roses all are dead that you have smelt;
You sit and laugh at men who loved your hair—
I sigh for dear dead kisses I have felt.

In this stanza the sentiment, the lilt, the imagery, are all the poet's own. It is possible that a careless reader would imagine that the lines were really addressed to some lady. We prefer to think—indeed, we are sure—that they were addressed to some seaside resort, whose identity is cunningly

[11]

veiled under the pseudonym of "Violet," lest Cromer or another should wax jealous. Surely it would be rather prosaic to speak of a lady's beauty as being "unimpaired." On the other hand, if we take it that, say, Broadstairs is apostrophised, then "not built over" would be the meaning, and the phrase would be felicitous and pretty. Surely, again, no lady, worthy of the name, would sit down on a chair and guffaw at men who had loved her hair, even though their proceeding had seemed ridiculous. We are sure that the *h* in "hair" is a conversational sort of *h*, dropped in to hide a sly reference to ozone. A popular seaside resort, moreover, can afford to "laugh" at the defection of a few visitors more or less.

From such lines as these, which do, indeed, offer many difficulties to the commentator, it is pleasant to turn to those simpler poems in which Scott bids God speed to those about to cross the Atlantic. "Look up, old boy," he says to Mr Brough,

> *our eyes their story tells,*
> *We have not come for weepings or farewells.*

Who but this dexterous artist could have thought of employing that emotional third-person-singular in the first line? Who, again, but he could have said, when Mr Hare was going to New York,

> *He came to us young, when the stage was deprest*
> *And needed his pruning, and lopping, and weeding,*
> *And alas! he now leaves us, of artists the best,*
> *A model of taste! the perfection of breeding?*

And who but he could have said, on a similar occasion,

> *And when we rise to heights supernal,*
> *We shall cry "Adsum!" like the Colonel?*

We must really husband our quotations. Yet we cannot

refrain from giving just one more. It is the last line of an elegy on Thomas Carlyle, and it is this:

Shut fast the gate! He's sleeping. Close the door!

There is no living man, save Scott, who could have written such poetry as this. But let it be understood that his valedictory or elegiac odes, marvellous though they are in their expression, are not the true, spontaneous outcome of his natural genius. His pen runs far more splendidly when it has been dipped, not in tears for the departing or the departed, but in those yet salter tears shed upon our coast by the eternal sea. Is it not a tragic thing that this poet should be chained in our metropolis, eating his heart out for the happier clime, escaping so seldom from his harsh bondage? The age of Patrons is past; else, surely, Lord De la Warr would ere now have insisted that Scott should live always near him in some little cottage at Bexhill-on-Sea. But the age of public generosity is not yet past. Only the other day, a Boy Poet was rescued from Silvertown, where, in some factory, he had been slaving. Between the life and work of Scott and of Curtice (was not that the Boy's name?) a close parallel might be drawn. Each is a poet of the same order, and we venture to assert that Curtice never wrote anything finer than has been written by Scott. Curtice was a plate-layer by trade. Scott is a dramatic critic. Why should the one be taken, the other left? The removal of the one has not affected the business of his factory. Quite prosaic hands can lay plates as well as his. Nor, we think, would the removal of the other damage our drama. His work could be done as well—nay! better—by prosaic hands. From the merely literary standpoint, his work is not good. He writes that always anomalous thing, a poet's prose, sadly plethoric and redundant. His column in the *Daily Telegraph* seems daily to topple down under its own weight. As criticism, his work is still worse. Cooped in the gilded confinement of a stage-box, Scott's soul becomes restless and intractable. The glare of the footlights blinds his clear, poetic vision. He gives such forcible expression to those feelings of friendship or enmity, gratitude or revenge—fine motives, mind you, for poetry!—as must be quite embarrassing to his admirers, and are even apt to mislead a public, notoriously unable to gauge the peculiarities of a poetic temperament. Nor is it from the drudgery of criticism alone that we would take him. Like Shelley and Tennyson, and how many others! he has essayed to write plays. Like them, he lacks the dramatist's touch. Unable to originate in this line, he has had to fall back upon adaptations from the drama of that city which once, in a patriotic spasm, he branded as "thoughtless Paris." That he should have dallied with that fair houri, Boulogne-on-Sea, is not to be wondered at. But Paris! "Thoughtless Paris!" An inland-town, too!

Now, we do earnestly appeal to the dramatic profession, ever generous in helping the oppressed, and not only to that profession, but also to all whose hearts have been, like ours, gladdened by the poetry of this man, to raise some great fund which will enable him to flee away, with his broken heart and his split infinitives, to the shores of Bexhill-on-Sea, there to work out his genius. It may be that his love for this place is not destined to be life-long. We suspect that Cromer was the great passion of his life. It is not given to any man to love twice with a devotion so ecstatic as that which Scott gave to Cromer. Perhaps he knows that that love is always really uppermost in his breast, and whispers, sometimes, to himself, in paraphrase of another poet:

I have forgot much, Cromer! Gone with the wind
And thrown confetti with the riotous throng,
Dancing to put thy red, lost poppies out of mind;
But I was desolate and sick of an old passion.
Yea! Though I wrote Bexhill up,—all along
I have been faithful to thee, Cromer! in my fashion.

[14]

But let us not pry into these heart-secrets. Let us, rather, respect the spoken wish of the poet. Scott has cried aloud for Bexhill-on-Sea. To Bexhill-on-Sea let him go. Poetry and Drama will uplift their voices in a sweet unison of praise, when they hear that he is, at length, living there. There, in commune with the works of Nature and Lord De la Warr, his soul will be purged, renewed, exalted. There he will forget, and will teach us also to forget, the bad part he once played in London. For "there's a retreat where," to quote once more his own wonderful words, he can "rest."

[*Saturday Review*, 12 September 1896. Unsigned]

Our Lady of "Pars"

T MIGHT BE ARGUED that Miss Marie Corelli is not quite a fit topic for discussion in a literary journal. Time was when the lady came to us regularly, in all her radiance, and we waved her courteously aside. Now she comes to us no longer. She is even as a coy mountain, and we go not to her. Indeed, to review books that one cannot read were both foolish and unfair. At the same time, only the veriest pedant could pretend not to be interested in the existence of one whose books, more popular than any in the market, do both soothe our cotters' evenings and grace the bedside tables of our princes. "Who is Connie Gilchrist?" was well enough in the disingenuous atmosphere of a law court. But such trifling is not for us. We know who Marie Corelli is, and we are not ashamed of our knowledge.

She represents very perfectly a new and interesting type. She is the prime product of the "Democracy of Letters." We are not quite sure what those three words, dear to the *Daily Chronicle*, exactly signify, but we take them as referring to certain new conditions imposed on literature by the spread of popular education. Formerly the illiterate could not read. But lately we (a national "we") have taught them to do so. In our simplicity, we had thought that English Literature would be enough for them to go on with, and with English Literature we stocked our public libraries. We were quite astonished when recent statistics showed us that the thing was a failure, for we had supposed that ability to spell out pages of type must surely create good taste. "What, then," we cried, "*do* the illiterate read?" Other statistics make answer. In the sale-lists of the booksellers we read the names of Hocking, Caine, du Maurier, Maclaren, Crockett, and Corelli; after each name certain appalling numerals. As we read them, we bow our heads.

The owners of all these names are good types of the "Democracy of Letters," but none may be mentioned in the same breath as Miss Corelli. None of them, but she, has quite forsworn allegiance to the old oligarchy of criticism. They still like their books to be reviewed. Not so she! She knows that the public needs no exhortation to read her. But she knows, also, that great masses are fickle to their favourites. She knows it to be essential that she should be always there, in person, before their eyes, whenever their eyes are not intent upon her printed pages. She rushes into their midst, a hunted thing, the uncowed quarry of Pressmen. She turns and faces her invisible pursuers. In wild accents she denounces them. With strong, small hands she rends them, and spurns them with an arched foot. Thus, and otherwise, does she keep her memory green. How crude, in comparison, are the other authors' bids for continued notoriety! Consider Mr Hall Caine! He, foolish fellow, must needs fare over the ocean and stump the States, sit for his photograph and profane the pulpits. His facial resemblance to Shakespeare (or Mr Swinburne, is it?) he cultivates with touching care, and there is not an interviewer but finds him chatty. Mr Maclaren, we are not surprised to hear, is also bound for America, and we suppose that Mr Crockett, too, not to be beaten, will soon take his little Sweetheart there. Now, we should have thought, seeing how very eulogistic and how very many are the reviews these gentlemen are fortunate enough to get, both here and in America, for their books, that the *rôle* of travelling cheap-jack was superfluous to their joyous being. We scarcely like to think of the fatigue and the expense that their ubiquity must entail. Of course, the Demagogues of Letters are the best judges of their own interests, but it were well perhaps if Mr Hall Caine and his rivals would take a well-earned rest now and again. If they

[17]

must rant in public, they need not go so far afield. Hyde Park is open to them, and tubs are quite cheap.

Quick, feminine intuition has helped Miss Corelli to avoid the mistakes made by these male demagogues. With far less exertion she can accomplish quite as much as, and even more than, they. Her effects in public life are gained with an economy of means that is astounding in so prolific a writer. She does not get herself reviewed. She does not lecture. She has never been a minister of the Presbyterian Church. And yet she is the subject of more paragraphs than any other living writer. By one simple and superb stroke of business she did more to advertise her books than she could have done by the diffusion of thousands of copies "for review." What man, woman, or child does not know that H.R.H. the Prince of Wales (future President, no doubt, of the Republic of Letters) "anticipated reading" one of Miss Corelli's books "with great pleasure"? When poor Mr Caine and his kind are not on the stump, their houses are positively infested with interviewers. "My door," says Miss Corelli, in a letter to the *Westminster Gazette*, "is rigorously closed to the paragraphist and the interviewer." A few words of scorn, hissed through the keyhole, are as much as these men are to expect. The very privacy of Miss Corelli's home becomes better copy than all the well-known details of Mr Crockett's den. Mr Crockett may perspire through all Scotland on his machine, and yet cause no more paragraphs than the young authoress who does "NOT ride a bicycle" and has "NOT invented a bicycle costume." In the infinite publicity of her seclusion, the very negativeness of Miss Corelli's tastes becomes stimulating to the world. She does "NOT shoot," nor has she "rented Killiecrankie Cottage for the 'shooting,' as there is none to speak of. It is a beautiful and idyllic little place, with exquisite grounds in which to rest or ramble, and where the birds have so little cause to be alarmed that the very robins fly in and out of the windows to be fed from my hand." Robins flying in and out of the windows and journal-

ists battering vainly at the doors! What a lesson to the other
Demagogues! We expect daily to hear from them that "they
have NO robins flying in and out of their windows." Indeed,
we would recommend those gentlemen to adopt the negative
form of advertisement suggested by Miss Corelli. It has infinite possibilities. Moreover, it would save them some
trouble.

Miss Corelli concludes her letter to the *Westminster* with
the usual hit at her critics and with another at Mr Max
Beerbohm, who, also intent on advertisement, replied to her
in the next issue. So is the ball kept rolling. Meanwhile,
Miss Corelli is "still misguided enough to prefer 'Poets'
Ideals' to blatant feminine vulgarities." And so are we.

[*Saturday Review*, 26 September 1896. Unsigned]

The Boat Race

THE VERY EARLIEST recollection of my life is bound up with an Oxford and Cambridge Boat Race. I was walking with my nurse along the Broad Walk in Kensington Gardens, and she stopped to talk to some other nurse, with whom, I suppose, she was acquainted. I remember that my nurse said "What are *you*?" and that the other nurse answered, "I am Cambridge." "Oh," rejoined my nurse, "I am Oxford." Not having yet seen more than three summers, I was too young to understand this elliptical mode of speech, and long after, whenever Oxford and Cambridge were mentioned in my presence, I thought that Oxford was my nurse, and Cambridge the other one. So deeply do things root themselves in the brain of a little child that even now, after the lapse of so many years, the names of the two great Universities do still vaguely suggest to me the image of these two nurses. And I attribute my early preference of Oxford to the notion I had that Oxford was *my* nurse. When the time came for me to choose the venue of my adolescence, how could I hesitate? Oxford received its sacred trust. Oxford moulded me. How petty, devious and remote are the details that inform a world's destiny!

Folly dies hard, and I gather from the newspapers that this Boat Race is not yet obsolete. The Thames is to be burdened with the usual contest, and haberdashers are hunting up *les rosettes d'antan*—I have never quite decided which colour is the more hideous—and all London is painfully excited. Even at this moment, in the Broad Walk, nurses stand discussing the chances and neglecting their charges. The butcher-boys can scarce contain themselves, and the very policeman has pinned a riband to the inside of his helmet. Why does this annual fervour pervade all London? At Oxford, the prospect of the race excites never more than a very mild interest; more interest, certainly, than the Chess Tournament, but far less than the Cricket Match at Lord's. Why then, here, this epidemic of Oxomania and Cambritis? Coming on the top of influenza, it is doubly dangerous, and I am sorry that no scientist has tried to discover the germ. It is hard to determine whether the infection spreads from the newspapers to the public or from the public to the newspapers. I incline to the former theory. The newspapers seem generally to succumb first. For some days, now, they have devoted an inordinate amount of their space to details about the dreary life which sixteen young men are leading at Putney. These young men are dieting themselves and living in accordance with a very strict regimen. They weigh themselves every morning, and, though their names are quite unknown to fame, every newspaper in London thinks it worth while to publish a list of their weights. I hope that these young valetudinarians will benefit by their change of air, but I cannot say that I find their condition interesting. I would suggest to them that, whilst taking excessive care of their bodies, they have paid too little attention to their minds. I have been glancing at the accounts of their daily diversions, which suggest imminent softening of the brain. When they are tired of rowing they stop to "shoot under Barnes Bridge." What game they expect to find there, heaven only knows. But, at least, this diversion is less lamentable than what follows. Conceive! Eight of the young men rowed some way down the river, followed by a crowd of solicitous friends on the bank. They got as far as Hammersmith. There they showed signs of exhaustion, and their friends advised them "not to overdo it." So they rested a little, and then, says the evening paper from which I am quoting, "from Hammersmith they paddled home." Is that the stuff of which modern England is to be made? Eight "men" students of a great

University, "heirs of all the ages, in the foremost ranks of time," get out of a boat, sit down on a bank at Hammersmith—at Hammersmith of all places!—take off their shoes and socks, and "paddle home." As a philosopher, I should like to have seen them.

I am not the first person who has been troubled by the fatuous side of the oarsman's life. In the 'seventies, Professor Ruskin, sitting in his Slade Chair, was troubled by it. As a practical man, he chafed at the utter inutility of rowing; he grudged so much energy its fruitlessness. As an enthusiast, he persuaded a score or so of able-bodied undergraduates, who would otherwise have fooled about on the river, to aid him in making a road. Wheel-barrows were wheeled about, pick-axes clove the earth, and there was, for a little time, a real, though limited, enthusiasm. Frost or fatigue or some other cause stopped them before very much had been accomplished. I am rather sorry. I, too, am a practical man, and it irritates me to think that at Oxford, throughout every term, they still throw so much energy into the Isis. I have often asked the rowers in College Boats whether they enjoy their life, and their answers have always been either negative or evasive. What fool's impulse drives a freshman to the river? If he row well, his whole life must be sacrificed to the pursuit. For the sake of his College, he must not smoke, nor eat and drink the things which are pleasant. After a fortnight's training for a race, every moment of his life ordered for him, the strongest man has an over-strained expression, resulting from an over-strained *physique*. His Spartanism is no more natural or healthy for an Englishman than would be the Oriental languor of divan and hookah. It is but a silly "deflection from the norm." When the days come for the races, the youth walks forth from the gate of his College, wearing the face of steadfast martyrdom. The stranger who passes by wonders what he is going to do, and follows curiously in his footsteps. "Surely," thinks the stranger, "some great thing is to be accomplished." The stranger sees him enter a barge by the river, soon to emerge, lightly-clad, with seven comrades. The stranger sees them all embark in a light skiff and notes that many gigantic muscles are swimming up and down their arms like dolphins in the sea. "They are strong," he thinks. "They are in a hurry. They are going somewhere." Yes. "What will they do there?" Nothing. "Will they ever return?" Presently. "What will they do then?" Nothing. Great pressure will have been brought to bear on the water.

Rivers have their uses. They are serviceable for purposes of commerce, scenery, suicide, and the like, but it is a shame that they should ever pass near a great University. So long as they do that, they are sure to encourage folly. The impulse towards rowing is, as I have suggested, essentially a fool's impulse. Perhaps that is why it is so generally felt. Or perhaps the average undergraduate is, like the hero of Mr Kipling's most famous story, the re-incarnation of a galley-slave. Galley-slaves have gone out of fashion, for war needs them not, nor commerce neither. Yet is their habit still among us. The shape of their boat has been altered, and the lash of the overseer survives only in the coach's blasphemies. Yet, strenuously, wearily, are true galley-slaves still plying oars through the water. And we, knowing how useless they are, do yet encourage them and call them heroes. Is it not time that we put a stop to their foolery? The University authorities are slow to move. But the Thames Conservancy seems to be a sensible sort of body, and why does it not forbid water-traffic to be impeded next Saturday on any account? To abolish the Boat Race would, I think, be an excellent way of commemorating Her Majesty's very long reign. But if the Boat Race cannot be abolished, surely, in honour of this great year, Cambridge might be allowed to win.   [*Daily Mail*, 27 March 1897]

At Cowes

I N ONE—I forget which—of Bulwer's novels there is a man who spends many years of his life in vain pursuit of an exquisite, mysterious lady, by him beloved. He traces her to Vienna, where he hears that she has just left for the Bosphorus. He reaches the Bosphorus, only to be told that her yacht has just sailed out of port, bound for the coast of Scotland. Off Orkney he almost comes up with her, but not quite. In Paris he misses her by five minutes, at Baden by as many seconds. The servants at her châlet in the Vosges Mountains inform him that she is even now on her way to some other place, where disappointment again awaits him. For me, I confess, the story of this interminable chase was as tedious as it was romantic, and save that it is rather analogous to my own chase of Fashion, I should not have recalled it. Aflame with social ambition, I am always just too late for every great and social congress. It is strange. A fortnight since I was staying within a stone's throw of Goodwood, whose glory had all departed hither. Now I am here, one of a not very select few. A fortnight or so hence I shall perhaps be able to start for Homburg, faint but pursuing.

Meanwhile, this is by no means my first visit to Cowes. I have often been here, but never so soon after the perihelion. In spring or late autumn I could enjoy myself very well here. The place itself is charming. The Squadron, with its thick battlements and its array of little brass cannons pointed across the Solent, gives one a sense of security from an English invasion, and, somehow, the Solent's water seems bluer, the sun more yellow, here than elsewhere. From the beach to the High Street everything is in miniature, and everything has a bright, sensible, little aspect of its own. I

cannot imagine a place less provocative of sad or subtle
thoughts. The smaller yachts, as they scud by, do not look at
all like white butterflies, and the larger yachts, when their
lamps are lighted at night and reflected in the dark waters,
do not remind one in the least of jewelled arks upheld by
slender, wavering columns of gold. Wherever you turn your
eyes, you catch an effect that is extraordinarily unlike a
Whistler. Yet, this year, I am dead to the ordinary charms
of Cowes. I walk dismally in the afterglow of fashion. I try
to distinguish in the waves' murmur some lingering echo of
the gaiety that has gone by. I cast my eye over the Squadron,
and with the aid of imagination and a few well-chosen cut-
tings from the columns of "Belle" and "Onlooker" I strive
to reconstruct the week before last—a faint, unsatisfying
panorama. Just opposite my window, at a distance of about a
quarter of a mile, there is what the uninitiated landsman
might take for a couple of large steamboats, with canary-
coloured funnels—in point of fact, the *Osborne* and the
Victoria and Albert. To the left there is a vast man-of-war,
which, lying there at anchor, means that the Queen is in
residence just beyond Old Castle Point. At the end of the
Osborne's deck is a little glass-house, and therein—not visible to us, but therein nevertheless—the Heir Apparent. All
day long the Parade is lined by Americans and others, looking through telescopes at the glittering panes of this pavilion.
The strongest lens reveals no glimpse of His Royal Highness,
but no one seems to despair—occasionally a field-glass, as
being easier to hold, is substituted for a telescope, but that is
the only sign of weariness shown by these loyal watchmen.
All day long, pinnaces, gigs, whatnots, emblazoned with the
three white feathers, pass to and fro between the yacht and
the landing-stages, objects of intense interest. The blue-
jackets that step out of them are cynosures—we know that
they have been near the rose, and we note that their faces
are tanned with reflected glory. To me there is something
strangely impressive in this sense of a great unseen presence,

a something not ourselves which yet directs and controls the hearts of us at all hours. Sometimes, with a little curl of smoke from one of her funnels, the *Osborne* moves from her moorings. The line of telescopes ashore quivers with excitement, as, slowly, majestically, she glides away. When she disappears behind one point or the other of the bay the reaction is almost intolerable. But she returns always before dinner-time. *Ruit oceano nox.* The Prince is in his yacht: all's right with the Roads. The little glass house glows with red-shaded lights. From it strains of music are wafted by the night-breezes—a harp, a fiddle, a human voice attuned to sentimental or comic melody—faint, certainly, by reason of the distance, yet clear and sweet, like all music heard across that sounding-board, water. Twice a week, in the evening, a band plays on the Parade. During "God bless the Prince of Wales" we all look towards the yacht, sure that those red-shaded lights illumine a duly-gratified smile. Never was so absolute an obsession. Gentle and simple have but one thought here, one topic: His Royal Highness. Were it known that I, I! had seen him with my own eyes, how I should be besieged! Seen him I have. How? On Monday night I was awoken from my first sleep by a flash of light and a terrific noise. I started from my bed and again, for an instant, my room was marvellously illuminated. I ran to the window, drawn thither by I know not what magnetism, knowing well that some strange thing would happen to me. The second peal of thunder had scarcely rattled into silence when again the darkness was wildly riven . . . I staggered back. I had seen the Prince at his window, I had caught his eye across the water, and—I had not bowed! . . . I waited for the next flash, tremulously. Quicker than the flash itself, I bowed; but, alas! the long-pent rain had begun to fall so densely that the yacht was a mere blur to me, and I knew that my bow was wasted.

Thus does unkind Fate trick us of the chances she dangles before our eyes. [*Saturday Review*, 20 August 1898]

"Tipping"

E ARE ALL AGREED in disgust of the system. "Tipping," we all say angrily, "is simply a form of blackmail." Of any commercial transaction that he dislikes the Englishman always predicates that it is simply a form of blackmail. Having expressed this formula in the "correspondence-columns" of a newspaper, he relapses into placid acquiescence, letting the blackmail be levied on him evermore. So long as he can publicly denounce a principle in what he would call "unmeasured terms," he is quite content to put up with the practice of it. His instinct is always to "ventilate," not to remove, grievances. The act of ventilation exhausts him of further initiative. And I think it a pity, therefore, that the vent of the correspondence columns in the public press should always be open to him. If he were docked of the privilege of seeing his own strong language printed in his own morning paper, he would probably seek relief in doing something to make such language unnecessary. If he could no longer proclaim, for the edification of the breakfast table, that he has watched this or that or the other thing with growing alarm; if he could no longer call it a sign of the times and say that the moment has come to make a determined stand against it; if he could no longer brand it as iniquitous, anomalous, ridiculous, indefensible from any point of view, reprehensible from every point of view, wholly intolerable, a scandal, a canker, a relic of barbarism, a disgrace to civilisation; if he could no longer rub his eyes and ask himself if he is living in the dark ages, and whether this is or is not a free country; if he could no longer (having concluded with a lurid prophecy of what will happen in the immediate future if this evil be not fearlessly stamped out, and with a frenzied appeal to all who call themselves citizens) inclose his card and remain, sir, your obedient servant, "Paterfamilias," or "Fiat Justitia," or "Civis Romanus Sum"—then, and (as he would say) not till then, there might be a chance of his making himself really useful. As it is, having inclosed his card and given himself a Latin pseudonym, he feels his whole duty accomplished. The card, somehow, is a charter of exemption from further trouble in the matter. The Latin pseudonym will so wing his words as to make them irresistible projectiles. A man once showed me a letter which he had written to a morning paper about the unpunctuality on the South-Eastern. (It is a curious, almost uncanny, sensation to see one of these people in the flesh.) His letter was signed "Indignans." To flatter his culture, I asked him what "Indignans" meant. "Indignant," he replied, gravely. "Oh, I see," said I; then, eager for light on a mystery which had always baffled me, I asked, "Why didn't you sign yourself 'Indignant'?" " 'Indignans' carries more weight," was his memorable answer. But I suspect that he did not really care whether his letter was likely to frighten the directors or not. That he had written it, and read it in print, was enough for him. He had duly rolled his thunder and flashed his lightning, and now the atmosphere of his soul was cleared to tranquillity. Anon, doubtless, he would be overclouded by some other grievance; but another detonation and fulmination in one of our ever receptive journals would forthwith enable him to forgive and forget it. Such is the manner of his kind. And his kind is that of the average man. And it is the average man who can only (by reason of his numerical advantage), if he will, effect reforms in things. And it is the "correspondence columns" that sap his will power. Therefore, I urge, those columns should be closed.

"Tipping" is a grievance most constantly ventilated. In and out of (the silly) season there are angry letters about it. This is the more deplorable for that it is a grievance which might be so easily removed. Railway companies have you at their mercy; it is better to arrive under their auspices an hour or so late at your destination than to walk the distance on foot. Only by arduous processes of legislation could you force them into punctuality. But the "tipping" evil is on quite another plane. It could be cured by the simple method of not giving "tips." Simple? Well, certainly, there would be a certain amount of moral courage involved. Merely to thank the porter who has put your luggage into the van, merely to compliment on his dignity the butler of a house in which you have been staying for a week, merely to say after dining in a restaurant "You wait well. You will go far" to the waiter who has just brought your change—to assume, in fact, that every labourer is worthy of his hire, and gets it from his employer, would demand of you a certain strength of character, *plus* a certain imposing firmness of demeanour, to enable you to get away without being insulted or importuned. At least, it would if you were acting as a single pioneer. But I do not advise anyone to act so. "Combine!" is my exhortation. Form a league; adopt some conspicuous badge. Let it be plain to the eyes of the whole world that there are no "tips" to be got out of *you*. You would not be waited on? Porters, butlers, waiters, chambermaids, gamekeepers, and all other folk who batten on the small change of the community, would turn deaf ears to your orders? They could not afford to do that. So obviously reasonable and attractive would your league be that, once formed, it would soon count among its members every single person of whom, at present, "tips" are expected. What would become of the porters and their kind? We know that in many fashionable restaurants the waiters actually have to pay the *restaurateurs*—have to buy the right of farming the "tips." We know that the same system is in force for the butlers and gamekeepers in the country-houses of the impoverished aristocracy.

In no hotel or restaurant or private household are servants

[29]

so paid as to make them independent of strangers' purses. The cutting off of their source of income would be a serious matter. But do not fear for them. They, too, would "combine"—quickly enough. Quickly enough their employers would be forced to pay them at a decent rate. Then all would be well. Travelling would be robbed for us of its chief drawback. Departure from one place to another would no longer be horrible. We should be spared those awful moments of meditation as to what is the smallest amount we can give without seeming miserly, that awful moment of false geniality when we bestow the "tip," that mortification if the recipient does not seem to be delighted, and that disgust at not having given less if the recipient does seem to be delighted. Everybody hates "tipping." To give spontaneously, in reward for some service rendered, to someone who expects nothing, may be very nice indeed. But to give because, in defiance of the laws of political economy, the employers will not pay the employed, is—well, it is simply a form of blackmail.

And now, having made my protest, I have exhausted my indignation against the system. The exhaustion is the more thorough for that I have made my protest, not in the form of a letter, but in such a way that I shall be paid for making it. And I have no doubt that most of the money due to me will be spent in the fashion condemned by me "in unmeasured terms."   [*Traveller*, 8 June 1901]

A Needed Noun

N THE MIDST of an essay, I find myself writing that So-and-so "was a great poet, but not a great writer of prose." Wishing to balance nicelier the antithesis, I pause, seeking some single word equivalent to those three words "writer of prose." Of course, I might change "poet" to "writer of poetry." But whoever has a sense of the value of anything—money, words, what not—is accordingly economical. Moreover, my space is limited. For the rest, "writer of poetry" strikes me as absurd. Yet not, indeed, as more absurd than "writer of prose." Surely, there must be some single word . . . I ring for a dictionary. . . .

"PROSER" (s.), a tedious speaker or writer." I shake my head.

"'PROSERPINA' . . . "PROSING (a.), talking or writing tediously." . . . "PROSLAVERY," and many other red herrings. . . . "PROSY (a.), like prose, dull and tedious." I raise my eyebrows. Why these repeated sneers at prose? Let me look at the definition of it. Turning back the page, I find "PROSE (s.), unmetrical or unrhymed (? unrimed) composition; ordinary language; (v.a.), to write in prose, to make a tedious relation." This is all very curious. "PROSAIC" catches my eye; "pertaining to prose; resembling prose; dull; uninteresting." And then "PROSAISM (s.), prose writing; mere prose." Poor prose! To have been weighed by Mr Nuttall in the balance and have been found dull, tedious, uninteresting, and mere! What is wrong with it? Or rather, what is wrong with Mr Nuttall's scales?

Of course, there is bad prose, even as there is bad poetry. And in prose, as in poetry, the quantity of good work is tiny in comparison with the quantity of bad work. Perhaps Mr Nuttall is (how could the maker of a popular dictionary not become) a man of gloomy temper? Perhaps he can perceive only the dark side of things? Let me find his definition of "POETIC." Doubtless, "pertaining to poetry; resembling poetry; sugary; insincere." . . . Yes, here we are: "pertaining to poetry; possessing"—what's this?—"the peculiar beauties of poetry; sublime." Dear me! And hear him on POETRY. . . . "The art of giving clear and rhythmic expression to forms which have been conceived in the fantasy with more or less of passion of soul and penetrative insight into reality." If that is not sunnily sympathetic, what is? Evidently Mr Nuttall is convinced that of the two generic forms in literature one must be enthroned and hymned, the other kicked. Why does he draw this weird distinction? Perhaps I am not quite fair to him. The maker of a popular dictionary must take the meanings of words as he finds them —as usage has made them. So let me absolve poor Mr Nuttall, and blame merely the public's usage, even as the priest at the door of the Tabernacle may sometimes have relented at sight of the harmless, hapless scapegoat, and have cursed in its stead the smug and naughty congregation.

One of the prices men have to pay for their egoistic natures is a tendency to glorify whatever they cannot do, and to contemn whatever they can do. Most men cannot write in rime and metre. Most men can, and often do, write without those frills. And so, whereas they revere poetry, for the unfrilled sister-form they have no reverence at all. Far it is from them to acknowledge that the common form is as susceptible of beauty as the rare one is. When they are confronted with a piece of prose to whose beauty they are not impermeable, they have this simple way out of their difficulty: "Oh," they cry, "this is not prose at all! This is poetry!" Thus, according to one of Mr Nuttall's subsidiary definitions, poetry is "any composition, whether in verse or prose, which is at once nobly fervid and vividly imaginative." In fact, you see, we must always hand over to poetry whatever treasure we may find in prose's possession. For can prose have come by any treasure honestly? Impossible! Such, at least, is the popular belief. One of its sources I have just shewn to you. But here is another. If prose were generally contemned for no other reason than that most men can write in it, this general contempt, which dates from time immemorial, would have arisen only with the general literacy produced by the late Mr Forster's famous Act. Human beings have always (except, perhaps, in time immemorial) possessed the faculty of speech. And they have always talked in prose. Thus, even before they could read or write prose, they were not much impressed by it. Because prose has always been talked, poetry has always been exalted as something apart, whilst prose has been bundled in with the common herd of things.

A fatuously drawn distinction! For, though it is harder to write bad poetry than to write bad prose, beautiful prose is as hardly written as is beautiful poetry. Hardlier, indeed. Prose is the unwieldier instrument. All the writers of good prose have written, from time to time, delightful verses. But few good poets have evolved two consecutive sentences of decent prose. I admit that not very many good poets seem to have attempted this evolution. Most of them, in their inflated pride, have disdained to write otherwise than "anyhow" in prose. But how few even of them who have respected their unusual medium have achieved through it any not feeble or grotesque result! Mr Nuttall's is not the only book that lies before me as I write. There is also the *Ulysses* of Mr Stephen Phillips (whom I may, without fear of embroiling myself in controversy, call a good poet). Obviously, the stage-directions throughout a play whose appeal is to the sense of beauty ought to be written beautifully. Else will the reader be jarred, even as in the theatre he would be jarred by some ugliness in that scenery or those dresses for which, in the book, these stage-directions are the substitute. Mr

[33]

Phillips, evidently, has realised this simple truth. He has tried, evidently, to make the prose of his stage-directions worthy of his blank verse. And yet in the forecourt of Ulysses' house, "*a wild scene of flinging fruits and red, white and purple flowers ensues.*" This little sentence (which I have taken at random) is so full of faults that one hardly knows how to begin a criticism of it. However . . . (1) "A scene of flinging fruits" is not grammar. (2) To "ensue," in the sense of to "follow," is a horrid vulgarism. (3) "Flowers ensues" is a horrid sibilation. (4) So short a verb as "ensues" ought not to have been separated so far from its substantive. It comes as an anticlimax at the end of the sentence; more especially so because it is a matter-of-fact word preceded by a number of picturesque words. (5) The punctuation is wrong, inasmuch as it does not follow the meaning of the sentence. Technically, it is all right. But that is not enough. If you read the sentence aloud, making no pause except at the comma after "red," the result is gibberish. Reading it to yourself, you see what it means, but with a consciousness of being jerked. As it stands, the sentence could not have been punctuated better; but for that reason, among many reasons, it should not have stood at all. A sentence that cannot be so punctuated that the reader shall be unconscious of the punctuation ought to be reconstructed altogether. (6)—But I have said enough to show you some of the differences between good prose and bad, and to convict Mr Phillips of writing here the latter kind in despite of his wish to write the former. Through blank verse he achieves a continuous effect of beauty; through prose, a continuous effect of cheapness. And, even as this stage-direction is typical of its fellows, so is Mr Phillips of his peers in poetry. They, like him, cannot write decent prose. Still less can they or he produce through prose an effect of beauty. And the reason is not that prose is less essentially than verse a medium for beauty, but because prose is the more difficult art. You remember Pater's advice to the young man who hankered after a prose

style? "Write poetry for the present: it is so much easier."
It is easier to stir the sense of beauty through poetry, because
therein you have the sensuous recurrence of appointed
rhythms, the sensuous accident of rimes. In prose, even as
you must eschew rimes, so you must eschew any regular and
explicit rhythms; and yet, without rhythm—rhythms that
beat time to its meaning—prose makes a quite vain appeal.
Sensibility to the subtle rhythms of prose is much more rare
than sensibility to the rhythms of poetry, even as blank
verse is less popular than rimed verse. (That is another
reason why poets are exalted above writers of prose.) But,
for those who have ears to hear them, these rhythms of prose
are as magical as the rhythms of poetry—more magical,
inasmuch as they are subtler and more rare.

Prose can achieve much that poetry cannot achieve—the
by-laws of the South-Eastern Railway Company, for example. But, for the true critic of literature, nothing that is
within the scope of poetry is beyond the scope of prose. What
poem in this language is more potent in its appeal through
beauty to emotion than is the prose of the Song of Solomon?
In its appeal through beauty to the reason, what poem is
more potent than is Pater's prosaic description of La Gio-
conda, or than his less famous, yet no less lovely, praise of
Botticelli's Madonnas, marred though that passage is by its
saliently iambic ending? The true critic of literature is as
grateful to the nineteenth century for its writers of prose as
for its poets. For by it the shackles which its predecessor had
riveted were filed off poetry and prose alike. Prose became,
by its grace, once more a medium for beauty. And yet, despite the noble work done by men so various as Ruskin and
Stevenson, Pater and Newman, one feels that the full glory
of prose, as a medium for beauty, was not realised by them—
is not yet realised, save by a few. Prose is not yet written as
frankly for its own sake as poetry. It ought to be. Of course,
I do not mean that it ought not to be continued as a vehicle
for every kind of didactic purpose. But it ought also to be

[35]

used, by those who could well use it so, for the expression of merely lyrical feeling. In modern English prose there are, it is true, many lyrical passages, but they are always sandwiched apologetically in the midst of expository writing. The only separate prose-lyrics that I can recall, written in English, are translations from another language—such as Mr Andrew Lang's translations from Theocritus. I recommend that dear little book as an incentive to young writers of prose. It will embolden them to be merely lyrical, thus hastening the day when writers of prose shall be as specific and distinct a class as poets are now, and when forty among the younger of them shall have a whole book of non-comparative criticism written about them by Mr William Archer.

In view of that glad day it is all the more needful that we should find some single word equivalent to "writer of prose." I have rejected "proser." *Prosers of the Younger Generation* would not do at all. But a second scrutiny of Mr Nuttall's pages has just revealed to me a word which I had overlooked. "PROSAIST (s.), a prose writer." Mr Nuttall, I regret to say, adds, "one who cannot rise above prose." But no matter. The word is too rare to have been imbued with a contemptuous significance. It is, to all intents and purposes, a new word. It is the very word I wanted. . . . And so, closing these intercalary reflections, I will return to my essay, take a new pen, and write that So-and-so was "a great poet but not a great prosaist. . . ." Yes, the word looks very well indeed. I shall use it often. May it pass into the currency.

[*Academy*, 8 February 1902]

A Lord of Language

HERE WAS A coincidence last week in London. An exhibition of Whistler's paintings was opened, and a book by Oscar Wilde was published; and all the critics are writing, and the gossips are gossiping, very glibly, about the greatness of Whistler, and about the greatness of Oscar Wilde. Whistler during the 'seventies and 'eighties, and Oscar Wilde during the 'eighties and early 'nineties, cut very prominent figures in London; and both were by the critics and the gossips regarded merely as clever *farceurs*. Both, apart from their prominence, were doing serious work; but neither was taken at all seriously. Neither was thanked. Whistler got a farthing damages, Oscar Wilde two years' hard labour. None of the critics or gossips took exception to either verdict. Time has rolled on. Both men are dead. A subtly apocalyptic thing, for critics and gossips (especially in England), is the tomb; and praises are by envious humanity sung the more easily when there is no chance that they will gratify the subjects of them. And so, very glibly, very blandly, we are all magnifying the two men whom we so lately belittled. M. Rodin was brought over to open the Whistler exhibition. Perhaps the nation will now commission him to do a statue of Oscar Wilde. *Il ne manque que ça.*

Some of the critics, wishing to reconcile present enthusiasm with past indifference, or with past obloquy, have been suggesting that *De Profundis* is quite unlike any previous work of Oscar Wilde—a quite sudden and unrelated phenomenon. Oscar Wilde, according to them, was gloriously transformed by incarceration. Their theory comprises two fallacies. The first fallacy is that Oscar Wilde had been mainly

[37]

remarkable for his wit. In point of fact, wit was the least important of his gifts. Primarily, he was a poet, with a life-long passion for beauty; and a philosopher, with a life-long passion for thought. His wit, and his humour (which was of an even finer quality than his wit), sprang from a very solid basis of seriousness, as all good wit or humour must. They were not essential to his genius; and, had they happened not to have been there at all, possibly his genius would, even while he himself was flourishing, have been recognised in England, where wisdom's passport is dullness, and gaiety of manner damns. The right way of depreciating Oscar Wilde would have been to say that, beautiful and profound though his ideas were, he never was a real person in contact with realities. He created his poetry, created his philosophy: neither sprang from his own soul, or from his own experience. His ideas were for the sake of ideas, his emotions for the sake of emotions. This, I take it, is just what Mr Robert Ross means, when, in his admirable introduction to *De Profundis* he speaks of Oscar Wilde as a man of "highly intellectual and artificial nature." Herein, too, I find the key to an old mystery: why Oscar Wilde, so saliently original a man, was so much influenced by the work of other writers; and why he, than who none was more fertile in invention, did sometimes stoop to plagiarism. If an idea was beautiful or profound, he cared not what it was, nor whether it was his or another's. In *De Profundis* was he, at length, expressing something that he really and truly felt? Is the book indeed a heart-cry? It is pronounced so by the aforesaid critics. There we have the second fallacy.

I think no discerning reader can but regard the book as essentially the artistic essay of an artist. Nothing seemed more likely than that Oscar Wilde, smitten down from his rosy-clouded pinnacle, and dragged through the mire, and cast among the flints, would be *diablement changé en route*. Yet lo! he was unchanged. He was still precisely himself. He was still playing with ideas, playing with emotions.

"There is only one thing left for me now," he writes, "absolute humility." And about humility he writes many beautiful and true things. And, doubtless, while he wrote them, he had the sensation of humility. Humble he was not. Emotion was not seeking outlet: emotion came through its own expression. The artist spoke, and the man obeyed. The attitude was struck, and the heart pulsated to it. Perhaps a Cardinal Archbishop, when he kneels to wash the feet of the beggars, is filled with humility, and revels in the experience. Such was Oscar Wilde's humility. It was the luxurious complement of pride. In *De Profundis*, for the most part, he is frankly proud—proud with the natural pride of a man so richly endowed as he, and arrogant with all his old peculiar arrogance. Even "from the depths" he condescended. Not merely for mankind was he condescending. He enjoyed the greater luxury of condescending to himself. Sometimes the condescension was from his present self to his old self; sometimes from his old self to his present self. Referring to the death of his mother, "I, once a lord of language," he says, "have no words in which to express my anguish and my shame." Straightway, he proceeds to revel in the survival of that lordship, and refutes in a fine passage his own dramatic plea of impotence. "She and my father had bequeathed to me a name they had made noble and honoured . . . I had disgraced that name eternally. I had made it a low byword among low people. I had given it to brutes that they might make it brutal, and to fools that they might turn it into folly. What I suffered then, and still suffer, is not for pen to write or paper to record." Yet pen wrote it, and paper recorded it, even so. And sorrow was turned to joy by the "lord of language."

"A lord of language." Certainly that was no idle boast. Fine as are the ideas and emotions in *De Profundis*, it is the actual writing—the mastery of prose—that most delights me. Except Ruskin in his prime, no modern writer has achieved through prose the limpid and lyrical effects that were achieved by Oscar Wilde. One does not seem to be reading a written thing. The words sing. There is nothing of that formality, that hard and cunning precision, which marks so much of the prose that we admire, and rightly admire. The meaning is artificial, but the expression is always magically natural and beautiful. The simple words seem to grow together like flowers. In his use of rhyme and metre, Oscar Wilde was academic—never at all decadent, by the way, as one critic has suggested. But the prose of *Intentions* and of his plays, and of his fairy-stories, was perfect in its lively and unstudied grace. It is a joy to find in this last prose of his the old power, all unmarred by the physical and mental torments that he had suffered.

Oscar Wilde was immutable. The fineness of the book as a personal document is in the revelation of a character so strong that no force of circumstance could change it, or even modify it. In prison Oscar Wilde was still himself—still with the same artistry in words, still with the same detachment from life. We see him here as the spectator of his own tragedy. His tragedy was great. It is one of the tragedies that will live always in romantic history. And the protagonist had an artist's joy in it. Be sure that in the dock of the Old Bailey, in his cell at Reading, on "the centre platform of Clapham Junction," where he stood "in convict dress, and handcuffed, for the world to look at," even while he suffered he was consoled by the realisation of his sufferings and of the magnitude of his tragedy. Looking joyously forward to his release, "I hope," he says, "to be able to recreate my creative faculty." It is a grim loss to our literature that the creative faculty, which prison-life had not yet extinguished in him, did not long survive his liberation. But, broken as he was thereafter, and powerless, and aimless, the invincible artist in him must have had pleasure in contemplation of himself draining the last bitter dregs of the cup that Fate had thrust on him.

[*Vanity Fair*, 2 March 1905]

[*On 16 October 1954, the centenary of Oscar Wilde's birth,
Sir Compton Mackenzie, after unveiling a plaque on Wilde's
house in Tite Street, Chelsea, read aloud this tribute by Max:*]

I suppose there are now few survivors among the people
who had the delight of hearing Oscar Wilde talk. Of these
I am one.

I have had the privilege of listening also to many other
masters of table-talk—Meredith and Swinburne, Edmund
Gosse and Henry James, Augustine Birrell and Arthur
Balfour, Gilbert Chesterton and Desmond MacCarthy and
Hilaire Belloc—all of them splendid in their own way. But
assuredly Oscar in *his* own way was the greatest of them all
—the most spontaneous and yet the most polished, the most
soothing and yet the most surprising.

That his talk was mostly a monologue was not his own
fault. His manners were very good; he was careful to give
his guests or his fellow guests many a conversational opening; but seldom did anyone respond with more than a very
few words. Nobody was willing to interrupt the music of so
magnificent a virtuoso. To have heard him consoled me for
not having heard Dr Johnson or Edmund Burke, Lord
Brougham or Sydney Smith.

Uniform Editions[1]

I HAVE A FRIEND who goes in strongly for uniform editions of modern authors; and very handsome these tomes do look on his shelves, to be sure—very monumental and memorial and definitive, and all the rest of it. I was staying in his house not long before the War; and one day, when he was out, I did something which, though not actually (I suppose) forbidden, argues a certain impudence in the doer: I took down one of the tomes and opened it. I was rewarded by the sight of a very noble page. *Richard Feverel* itself is a very noble book. I had read it in more than one edition—more than one casual, inconspicuous, unassuming edition. Gazing at the volume in my hand, I wondered whether any one but a giant who was also very rich would be able to read it without self-consciousness: without book-consciousness; and with an illusion that the story was of things that had happened. I turned to that well-remembered chapter, "A Diversion on a Penny Whistle;" and presently, taking a pencil from the writing-table, wrote opposite to the title-page of the splendid volume:

> *"Here lie the bones of Richard Feverel."*
> *"Have you any other editions?" "Several."*
> *"Then I'd rather have one of* them, *please. I've*
> *A sort of a feeling for Richard alive."*

One poem leads to another. In a volume of the Henry James set possessed by my friend these lines, unbeknown to him, occur:

[1] Published in 1922 as an introduction to *The Works of Max Beerbohm*, the first volume in the limited edition of Max's collected works.

Here fair young Daisy Miller lies.
O, Speculator, pass not by!
What though her spirit will not rise?
Her tomb's price will, quite possibly.

And if my friend (throwing custom and propriety to the winds) will look into the first volume of his Stevenson set, he will find:

"Ci-gît—who? You'll never guess!"
"Gibbon perhaps?" "No; R.L.S."
"He?—that blithe adventurer? He?
Well, poor fellow, R.I.P."

I am afraid I scribbled other verses in other sets also. But even thus I was not rid of my spleen. I thought I would express for publication my sense of the wrongness of these uniform editions. I sat down, pondered, and began to write a rather ambitious trialogue. Apollo therein pleaded that books had their own souls as well as their own destinies, that the various books of any one writer had quite separate souls, and that these all perished alike when their bodies were caught and forced into equal dimensions. Procrustes argued earnestly against this view of the matter. He was rebuked by Midas for saying that he cared not whether the bodies were all big or all little so long as they were all quite even. Great size, said the king, was as necessary as great gorgeousness. This infuriated Apollo. Gorgeousness and bigness the god declared to be as bad, from the literary standpoint, as uniformity itself. Better, said he, any old battered and tattered array of third and fourth editions (for in them the souls were abiding still) than one of these great stark staring regiments of inhuman monsters dressed up to the nines. There is no doubt that Apollo was going to get very much the best of the argument. But an idea, an odd vague possibility, had floated into my mind. Suppose that some day in

[43]

the far future I, even I, were asked to—to . . . most unlikely, of course; yet unlikely things had been known to
happen . . . and it must be rather gratifying to be asked
to assent to the bringing-out of a—a . . . and one might
even want to assent . . . and how could one not refuse
abruptly if one had declared at large an abhorrence of all
other such publications? Thus idly reasoning, I crumpled up
my trialogue and dropped it into the waste-paper basket;
but I was careful to laugh at myself for doing so.

And one day in the autumn of 1919 I laughed quite
spontaneously when dear William Heinemann of a sudden
suggested to me that an uniform edition of me would not be
amiss. He told me that the idea was not his own—had been
conceived by Mr Macrae, of the firm of Dutton & Co., New
York. He said the proposal was that Messrs Dutton should
publish one such edition of me over there, and he another
such edition over here. Also, I remember, he showed me a
letter in which Mr Macrae spoke of me as "that splendid
old lion, Max Beerbohm." That I was old I knew. That I
was splendid and leonine was a revelation; dazzled by the
light of which I made a feebler resistance than I should
otherwise have made to the whole scheme. No matter. I
should anyway have yielded in the end. Nor had I so lost
my head that I forgot to make certain conditions. The volumes must, I said, be as modest in size as they would be few
in number. They must be in physical proportion to the spirit
and ambition of the writer. Also, their aspect must be of a
simple-gay kind, as opposed to the ornate-dismal. And
though, of course, they would all have to be equal in height,
let them at any rate be all of different colours, so that here-
after on shelves every one of them should seem not to have
lost utterly its own little soul. Heinemann was always re-
luctant to oppose even a bad idea if it came from a writer
whose work he liked. Any good idea from such a source he
welcomed with the utmost of his eagerness and animation.
Within a few days he had already put into rough practical

shape the scheme we had discussed. The task seemed to amuse and please him. And for me this set of volumes will always be closely associated with his memory.

One of the principles in which he concurred with me was that there should be no "re-writing." When my first volume of essays was published I was but twenty-three years old. Possibly I have improved since then. Possibly I have deteriorated. Assuredly I am different. Why should I try to put my old head upon the shoulders of a young man in the distance? There are, I know, august modern precedents for attempting this operation. But I have attempted it not. I conscientiously object to it. The young man in the distance (though I admit that in many ways he irritates me) does not deserve to be beheaded. And would he not have a fair grievance against me even if I were surgeon enough not to kill him outright, and could by a wondrous feat of grafting make him artificially survive as half-a-fogey? It seems to me that the reader of these volumes would also have just cause for complaint. The growth or decline of any human being, however uninteresting he may in himself be, is not uninteresting, surely. It is a process quite good to watch. I have not tried to prevent you from watching it in the four volumes of essays that form the first instalment of this uniform edition.

The young coxcomb in the distance, t'other side the gulf of five-and-twenty years, stands intact. I have but, as it were, signalled to him that there were slight defects here and there in his toilet. Reading my book of 1896, I found some faults of grammar, even of spelling. These I have dared to amend. I found also sentences in which, through inexperience or carelessness, I had failed to make clear my meaning. These I have presumed to remodel (but piously, in a style consistent with mine of all those years ago). Punctuation is (or should be) almost as personal a matter as selection of words; but there are certain fixed general laws about it which everybody must obey; and at the age of

[45]

twenty-three I didn't obey all those laws, for I didn't know them all. Wherever I have found a positive blunder in punctuation, I have put it right. But the *style* of the punctuation I have nowhere altered. Altogether, I have behaved with much tact and forbearance; and I hope that my old self is grateful to me.

It would seem that in the three years that elapsed between his first and second book of essays my old self took lessons in spelling and in grammar. Also, his punctuation became professional (without, thank heaven! ceasing to be his own). In *More*, accordingly, the changes made by me are even fewer and slighter than in *The Works*. The third book, *Yet Again*, was published in 1909; and I do not feel that its author is very remote from me. His outlook on life and his way of writing are not mine; but they are not unlike mine. He and I are on fairly familiar terms; and the author of *And Even Now* has not felt that he was taking any liberty in deleting here and there from *Yet Again* a sentence that seemed to him stupid. He has even added here and there a sentence that seemed to him clever. Perhaps he ought not to have done that. But who can always follow exactly the rules he has laid down for his own guidance?

Rapallo, 1921

"Mr Punch"[1]

HERE IS HE? He was born in the land of my adoption, Italy; but I never come across him here. He is known to have travelled in France during the days of the Grand Monarque; but there's never a trace of him in France now. And even in England, which was so very much the land of *his* adoption, he is seen no more, and survives only as a name, the name of a well-conducted periodical. Tell me where he is, and I will follow him, for old sake's sake, to the ends of the earth. He cannot have gone to Heaven. His record was so very black. Somewhere he must have founded a colony—perhaps with the muffin-man and the lamp-lighter and other fascinating worthies of dim old Victorian London.

The last time I saw him was on a late afternoon in the November of 1915, at the corner of a side-street in Marylebone. I had been drawn to the spot by the sound of a voice that was—surely?—his, a squeaking and a strident voice that was yet sweet to one who for many years had not heard it and had hardly thought to hear it again. There my old friend was, yes, aloft in his booth, wagging from side to side, with his cudgel cuddled to his gaudy though shabby breast, talking eloquently to me of my childhood. And there was poor Toby, as bored as ever, and as ashamed of his absurd collar, but conscientiously barking at the Beadle and at those other persons of the play—barking above the sound of the drum and reed-pipe of the traditional man in front, though never above the sound of his master's voice. Not very many miles away, the War was being fought; the news

1 Published in 1923 as an introduction to *The Tragedy of Mr Punch* by Russell Thorndike and Reginald Arkell.

was not good, and the future obscure. But the survival of Punch in our changed city and in our tragic world seemed to be somehow an earnest of England's invincibility. His small audience of small boys did not, however, appear to be relishing his antics as the children of my day did. He was a stranger to them, I take it. And mostly, perhaps, they were Boy Scouts, trained to do a good action every day; so that this wife-beater, with his homicidal and infanticidal ways, rather shocked them. But I, less well-brought-up, was wholly unoffended; and I lingered after the close of the performance to give to the two men (who, I tried to think, reminded me of Codlin and Short) what sixpences I had on me. The elder said they had a very hard time to keep going —though there was no competition to stand up to: "me and him are about the last of the Punch and Judy men." He gave it as his opinion that the show was out of date. "But," he added a moment later, "it *is good fun* still, guvnor, don't you think?"

A very old gentleman to whom on the following day I related this incident surprised me by showing no sympathy at all; and the reason for his apathy surprised me still more. He had detested Punch and Judy shows ever since the introduction of a real dog as Toby. In his childhood, Toby had always been a small painted wooden dog. The change had, I gathered, been fatal to the virtue of the production. I admitted that the animate Toby had rather a dog's life; but the old gentleman did not object on grounds of humanity: he resented merely the breach of a sacred tradition. It occurred to me that old gentlemen are rather childish. But it also occurred to me that this might be truly said of middle-aged men too. And, furthermore, were not children themselves rather like old gentlemen? I remembered that when I was about nine years old I attended a juvenile party at which there was a Punch and Judy show, and how deeply that show puzzled me and jarred on me. Indoors!—and all so spick and span! The green baize curtains brand-new, unfaded by rain, unstirred by any gust of wind; and Punch, that greatly weather-beaten veteran, as fresh as a good girl's wax doll! To my crabbed and crusted mind all this was very repellent. But I cannot blame myself for my disgust at certain liberties that had been taken with the play itself. Punch was not really wicked: he was only, it appeared, naughty. The Beadle was not killed; Judy was not killed; even the baby was only hurt by its fall. Punch was not left hoity-toitying over a world in which he was gloriously sole survivor. He did not succeed in hanging the hangman, and himself escaped the noose only on promising in lachrymose falsetto that he would not be naughty any more.

Drama for babes, that; not for boys—at any rate in the Pre-Scout era. It was as though the Clown in the harlequinade (Punch's nephew) were to go about with a lukewarm poker and presently surrender even that at the bidding of the Policeman. It is long since I went to a pantomime; but I am told that the harlequinade has been whittled away to almost nothing. Soon, I daresay, the Clown (unable to stand the cold stare of the virtuous young) will have sailed away to peg out a claim in the colony founded by his poor old uncle. Will Falstaff, his cousin, have to go too? Perhaps not. Falstaff addresses himself only to adults; and adults are wayward and not easily shocked. I submit Mr George Robey as a proof of their unregeneracy. Here is a lineal descendant of Punch. I believe that off the stage he is a most estimable citizen. But *on* it? No civic virtue about him there! There, like his ancestor and the rest of the family, he spurns and tramples on the proprieties of our commonwealth. Observe the curl of his moist and mobile lip; and the glare of his unabashed and rolling eye. The very contours of that full bare throat are insolent. That costume is a manifesto of contempt for our opinion. Here is an overman of the underworld; lording it over us too, with a kind of hostile unction. Would we have him other than he is?

A thousand times, No. Who, among adults, can resist the charmless charm of him?—who not desire that he shall go on flourishing always exactly as he is?

"This is a moral world." Agreed. "Conduct is three fourths of life." Granted. Without the checks imposed on us by sense of right and wrong, and by fear of consequences, the world would very soon collapse. But the instinct to behave well was not in mankind at the outset. Mankind had to evolve it and cultivate it—and hasn't even now got enough of it to insure the future definitely. The more we are frightened, the better for us. Preachers, please note. But however much we may improve, however many new leaves we may turn over (and not hark back), I suppose there never will be a time when we shall not now and again need to imagine all our dismal old restrictions and inhibitions being kicked gaily about by some unscrupulous and overweening creature who goes all unpunished for doing so and indeed thrives immensely on so doing. We don't even now want to see anything of the sort in real life. But to have something of the sort presented to us on the plane of art is a natural craving. And that craving should not be starved. To satisfy it is to provide a wholesome vent for emotions which would otherwise be mischievous. Mr Robey is a great force for good. But he is mortal, he cannot last forever. Where, I repeat, is his immortal forbear?

What an odd coincidence! At the very moment when I had finished the foregoing paragraph, a friend laid on my table a little book entitled *The Tragedy of Mr Punch*. It is by Russell Thorndike and Reginald Arkell, and was published last year; and my friend tells me that an enlarged and illustrated edition of it will appear before Christmas. I have just been reading it. And it answers the question that I have twice asked. *Here* Punch is. I extend to him the heartiest of welcomes. He has not changed at all, thank Heaven!—is every bit as young in spirit and old in sin as ever he was in the palmiest of Victorian and other days; and I detect not a

[50]

hint of colonial accent in the fondly-remembered lingo that he utters. I thank his two sponsors for having so piously brought him back unscathed into civilised society. They whisper to me that he is *not* unscathed. They have a theory that he is inwardly raging because he only makes us laugh. It is an ingenious theory, and I delight in it for that reason. But I should be distressed if I were convinced by it. That radiant fixed smile—does it really conceal a secret sorrow? Rather do I think it is the frank glad smile of a great sinner well-knowing himself to be also a great force for good.

Rapallo, 1923

William Archer

AY AN OLD FRIEND of William Archer add to the admirable account that you have given of him as critic a few words of more personal memory?

I would wish to utter these because Archer was not, I think, very well understood by the many people who had the pleasure of mere acquaintance with him. To acquire the pleasure of his friendship was a rather arduous task. The rigidity of his style in writing showed itself also in his social "form." He was extremely Scottish in manner, and his shyness was unaccompanied by that uncertainty of demeanour which makes shyness charming at once. His voice was rather hard; his face (that handsome, aquiline face of his) lacked expression; his whole body was inexpressive. You guessed, if you were intuitive, that he had an emotional nature; but it would take you some years to prove this startling notion. He never reacted to the stimulus of convivial moments. I remember him at a banquet given to Holger Drachmann, the Danish poet and dramatist, some twenty years ago in London. Mr Gosse was felicitous chairman, and the huge, venerable, Vikingly guest made a Vikingly oration that moved the diners to paroxysms of enthusiasm. Few of us had read him, but we knew that Archer must have done so, and we called loudly for a speech from Archer. He conscientiously rose; he said (pronouncing the illustrious name as though it rhymed to black man) that he had that morning been reading Herr Drachmann's latest play, and had "found much to admire in it," and gave just such a chastely favourable account of it as he would have given in the daily or weekly Press. Nothing, I am sure, could have chilled the Northern glow of our guest's great heart, but we others experienced with dismay the steadying of our pulses, and felt almost as though we had only been having breakfast. We should have reflected that one of the points differentiating Archer from most of us was that he would willingly before breakfast or after dinner take any amount of trouble to do Herr Drachmann or any other deserving person a practical service. He was ever an indefatigably unselfish man.

But zeal for the deserving is quite compatible with coldness of nature. Archer's great charm was in that genuine warmth of feeling which, by perseverance, some of us were able to discover. That he had not, and did not want, a great number of friends, made his friendship the dearer to us, made us the prouder of having it. We valued it also as a means of enjoying his deep sense of fun and humour. This was a thing unrevealed in his criticisms of plays or books. He somehow could not fit it into his style (except indeed when he was conducting one of his many controversies: then, certainly, he abounded in playfulness which, with his perfect temper and steely grasp, made him the least desirable of antagonists). It was in conversation with his friends and in letters to them—letters of a sprawling penmanship which would surely have misled any graphologist—that something almost rollicking came out; and this we appreciated all the more because we never grew quite used to it.

Nobody was more amused than he by that irony of fate which, after so many years of his earnest theorisings about drama, suddenly tossed him up as writer of a vastly popular play. All his friends were tickled by that, but they were, even more, pleased for Archer. They liked to think of him enjoying his "little old age pension," as he called it, for many years to come. Would that fate's irony had not deprived Archer of those years—and us of Archer!

[*The Times*, 6 January 1925. Unsigned]

William Rothenstein[1]

OT LONG AGO I was looking through a few of some hundreds of letters that I have kept; and among those which I paused over, and mused and smiled over, was a note sent to me at Oxford, in the Summer Term of 1893, by a Christ Church man. The writer wanted me to dine with him on the following Tuesday, "To meet a young painter" who had just arrived from Paris. The prospective host had not yet seen him, but "his name is Rothenstein." And there was a postscript: "I understand that he speaks English perfectly."

But for that assurance, I might not have accepted the invitation. Nor, but for my belief that the small, dark, unhesitating man whom in due course I met was a stranger to our shores, might I have been so astounded as I was by his ease and mastery. There were four or five other guests, and all, I fancy, had come prepared to help a lame dog over a stile. Instead of which they found themselves trying to keep pace with the thoughts of a thinker and the *mots* of a wit who couldn't have seemed more at home on his own shores —whatever those shores might be. Withal, young, obviously, in years—as young as any of us. How very callow the elder members of the party seemed beside him! mere children, new-born babes even. One of the younger ones wrote in recent times a fantastic story in which the effect of Will Rothenstein upon the undergraduates (and dons) of Oxford was incidentally described. I can testify that the writer did not exaggerate what was felt. It was awe. Joy was mingled with it, of course, but—an awful joy which some-

[1] Published in 1926 as an introduction to *The Portrait Drawings of William Rothenstein 1889–1925, An iconography* by John Rothenstein.

how didn't become less awful when we found that our visitor was a native of Great Britain.

For one who lives usually, as I do, rather far from the land of his birth, the force of old first impressions is even greater than it is for most men; and my instinct is ever to think of my old friend Will not as a Professor out there in South Kensington, with multitudes of rapt pupils day by day, and with already a vast quantity of paintings and drawings done and now hoarded in private collections or flaunted in public galleries, but as a very young man with just the world before him, and Oxford for a few weeks agape in the meantime. This habit could have no more violent corrective than the sheaves that lie before me—proof-sheets of a monumental iconography composed in filial piety by a grown-up son.

The reason why these lie before me is no shock to me. Never parted from myself, I am well aware that I am quite old enough to be invited to write a few words for such a volume. My bother is that the years in their passage have not at all qualified me to perform the task worthily. Perhaps indeed the years' failure is the reason why I was chosen. The choice of introducer cannot have been an easy one. I imagine the son saying, "Father, does the Archbishop of Canterbury know much about graphic art?" and the father replying, "My child, there must ever be value in any opinions held on any subject by a man of wide spiritual experience. But already the massiveness of the temple that you have reared in my honour oppresses me rather. Get that frivolous young thing, Max Beerbohm, to come and throw some somersaults on the steps of this great edifice." I imagine the son pointing out that I am no longer young or frivolous or agile, and the father realising the truth of this, but saying, "No matter. At any rate he's undignified." So here I am. But fuller of awe than ever.

"Awe" is just what Will, in a prefatory note to the catalogue of a recent exhibition of early drawings by him, has said that he felt for some of those famous elders who sat to him in the days that I recall. I was not present at those sittings, and had supposed, rather, from his comments on those gods, that some such phrase as "acute intellectual curiosity" would have met the case. About Whistler, of whom in Paris he had been seeing much, he was wont to speak with more or less bated breath. But acquaintance with that sharp and blithe, that "wicked" and wonderful but not altogether inimitable old spirit was unlikely to foster in any lad a generalised sense of reverence for the reverend. I am inclined to think that the awe of which Will is now conscious was only subconscious at the time when those drawings were done. It was there, right enough, but not very obtrusive—even in the drawings. It was there because Will, despite his natural high spirits, and despite the temporary influence of Whistler upon the outlook of all striplings who passed by, was a man of essentially sober intellect. One sometimes realised this, even then. I remember an evening at the Café Royal (can we greybeards *never* set pen to paper without remembering some evening at the Café Royal?) when Oscar Wilde, who had for some time been talking in a vein of iridescent nonsense about some important matter, paused and said, with good reason and with genuine feeling, "My dear Will, don't look so serious!" It was not often that the sobriety of my friend's intellect exposed itself in those days. But the intellect itself was forever to the fore, and not less in his work than in his talk.

His work during the past thirty years and more has been very various, both in medium and in subject-matter. But it has always had the common denominator of his intellectual force; and this force is also, I think, the outstanding and governing factor in it. Even if he be painting a barn or a tree, a cart or a hedgerow, he seems to be saying, "What *is* this object? Just what part does it play among the eternal verities? And just how can I pluck the heart out of it?" I cannot pretend to answer such questions, I edge away to ground on which I feel safer—though far from secure. Caricaturists (and I am of that lowly tribe) are in some sort students of human character through the human form. They are rather more able than most people to appreciate what the serious portraitist is out for and up to. And it is to portraiture more than any other single kind of work that Will Rothenstein has devoted his unceasing energy.

In portraiture, as in other forms of drawing and painting, a good deal can be achieved with very slight expenditure of brain-power. The brain may be hardly more than the transmitter of messages from the eager eyes to the well-trained hand (via the pure warm heart); and if it transmit these accurately, the result will be delightful, and in some cases—such as that of the latest debutante or a very young Master of Hounds—satisfactory. Nevertheless, an artist who is nothing but sensitive and skilful must, I am sure, feel much happier sitting on a camp-stool and doing a landscape than when he is confronted with even the most meaningless of human sitters. Brains are an advantage to the landscape painter; but a fine landscape can be done without their assistance; whereas in the doing of a fine portrait they are as needful as sensibility and skill—aye! even in portrayal of a quite null person, inasmuch as without a profound statement of that nullity the portrait, though it be satisfactory for a while, will soon pall.

With the faces of quite null persons Will has dealt more frequently than I had supposed before seeing this iconography. (None of these is represented here, nor will I give the numbers of the pages on which their owners' names occur: I will merely say that, to the best of my recollection, profundity of statement was not stinted.) But the striking thing is the enormous number of truly distinguished persons here enshrined. That impulse which first whirled Will up to Oxford, the impulse to do a "set" of the people who mattered most in a place that matters much, has never since loosened its hold on him. Celebrities come and go. Celebrities leave Will cold—unless they be something more than celebrated. Distinction is what he likes; and if it be coupled with obscurity, no matter: there it is, and all the better perhaps. There is something almost snobbish in Will's austere freedom from snobbery. Private nullity he will patiently record. To the public kind he is adamant. One is guilty of the weakness of shedding a tear for those famous men whose names are *not* here enshrined. They have been judged and found wanting. True, the sentence passed upon them is merely negative. It is not, however, the less heavy. One wishes the judge could be induced to reconsider his—but no! Let not our sentimentalism try to tamper with his righteousness and rightness. Let posterity have all untainted (but for the queer inclusion of myself) this august record of what has been best among us in our time.

What would we not give to possess a similar record of . . . oh, the pitfalls that abound for unwary writers! I was about to say "the men of Johnson's time," quite forgetting Sir Joshua. Will some scribbler in the next century be on the point of forgetting Will? Sir Joshua's gift, like my friend's, was primarily intellectual, but (and hence, perhaps, the narrow shave I had a moment ago) Sir Joshua was of worldlier fibre, and a merely pretty lady or merely fine gentleman was safe, in his hands, from "profundity of statement." Indeed, these were the sitters he most tended to, good easy man. But outside that enchanting galaxy were certain other persons, his particular friends, his peers, on depiction of whom he honestly, and with passion, lavished the fulness of his power. Such men as Johnson or Burke or Goldsmith sounded the depth of him, and he of them. It is a pity that no painter had Reynolds's mental calibre in the days of Byron and Shelley. A little later came the drawings of Maclise. Let us be grateful for those lucid and gay presentments of the men that flourished around *Fraser's Magazine*. But Maclise was only a light-weight. The back-view of Bulwer making his toilet before a cheval-glass is all we need;

but the front-view of old S. T. Coleridge leaning on his stick
tells us little, where so much was to be told. Many of the
later Victorians had the advantage of G. F. Watts's fine and
disinterested attention; but this advantage was not great.
Watts himself, though in a way very different from Maclise,
was a light-weight; he was ethereal, and saw Browning and
all those other massive persons of his day as spirits already
in Heaven, at peace there, behind a golden haze which today gives one a sense of difficulty in finding one's way around
the room devoted to them by the Trustees of the National
Portrait Gallery. While Mr Sargent, that great master, was
living, I often wondered that he did not make, as he so well
might have made, a point of selecting only such sitters as
were worthy of him. He was definitely "an intellectual," and
no man was a greater respecter or better discriminator of
intellect. Also, he was intensely fastidious, in literature, in
music, in all things. How many a canvas or sheet of paper
testifies to his dislike of the vapidity or vulgarity of the lady
or gentleman at his mercy! He certainly relieved his feelings. But why should he have let his feelings suffer so
often? With what joy he could rise to a great occasion is
shown by his portrait of Coventry Patmore. I never saw that
sitter; but no matter: there he is, the author of all his works,
the entire man, body and soul. That picture was done many
years ago, before Mr Sargent began to dislike portrait-
painting. In later years, when a great occasion came his way
he did not always rise to it. No man was a greater devotee or
more acute appreciator of the writings of Henry James. And
certainly no portrait could be superficially more like Henry
James than was the portrait that his friend painted for his
seventieth birthday. But it will rather puzzle the students
of that writer's work in future ages; whereas the sight,
for a few minutes, of the man himself would have satisfied
them as completely as the portrait of Patmore satisfies
me.

I tell them that at the time when Will Rothenstein did the

lithograph that is reproduced in this volume Henry James's head was less magnificently characteristic than it became in his old age. But they will not listen to me: "This," I hear them saying, "is assuredly the man we know, poor troubled soul, hesitating in all sorts of agony before he takes the deep dark plunge into his 'later manner'." And assuredly it is. The greater the chance, it seems to me as I look through these drawings, the firmer is Will Rothenstein's grasp of it. And the older he grows, it also seems to me, the firmer the grasp becomes. The drawing of Lord Balfour is one of many that lead me to suppose that a drawing of Henry James in later years would have probed even further and more finely than this early one. The artist's vision of his sitters has in its strength a greater delicacy than of yore. There is more of sympathy now in the sure understanding. That quality of "awe" which in the old days was, as I have said, not apparent, does now appear—and appears not less clearly in the portraits of quite young men than in those of men whose very years would suffice to make them venerable. I remember that Aubrey Beardsley delighted greatly in the pastel that you will see here. The wit of it was very congenial to his taste. But he might have liked it less could he have foreseen how Will would be drawing the marvellous boys of a later era. The change is extremely interesting. And the technical method of draughtsmanship has of course changed also, in accordance to the deepening and mellowing of spirit. It is a beautifully right method for one whose way now is to seek out truth by seeking out what is best.

I trust that Will's faculty for awe will never develop so far as to prevent his fingers from putting pencil to paper. I reassure myself that if anything of the sort seemed likely to occur the fierce spirit of youth would rise again in him and adjust matters. And I like to think that thirty years hence there will be sitting in his studio a small man with a patriarchal white beard, saying in "perfect English" as many stimulating things as ever while he records with just the requisite amount of awe the faces and characters of distinguished youths unborn at the moment when I write these words.

Pistoia, 19 August 1925

Fantasy in Costume
Points Raised by an Opera Hat[1]

USED TO LIVE in London. I was even born there. I took the whole place as a matter of course. But now I live more than six hundred miles away from it; and my visits to it are as those of a simple, gaping, alien sight-seer. A note of scarlet is struck by the Baedeker that I bear through your grey thoroughfares.

I was last there in the Spring of 1925; and one of the sights made a quite ineffaceable impression on me, though I had but a glimpse of it. I was in a taxi-cab, and had asked the driver to go quickly as I was late for dinner at a friend's house. Through the open window of my vehicle I saw thus only for an instant my old friends, those two distinguished brothers in art, Charles Ricketts and Charles Shannon, walking together, and though I waved my hand wildly to them they did not see me. At any rate, Shannon did not. Ricketts may have, perhaps, and just ignored me. For I was not wearing a top-hat. And Ricketts was.

I saw him with it on. Moreover, it was an opera hat—a gibus, a chapeau-bras—a thing that opens with a loud plop and closes with a quiet snap; old-world emblem of the frivolous and the mundane, the light and worthless.

Wondrous enough to me, on the fine head of Ricketts, would have been a top-hat for use by daylight only. Thirty years ago everybody, except Ricketts, and with him Shannon, sometimes wore a hat of that kind. Indeed, most of us

[1] Published in 1928 in *Robes of Thespis*, Costume Designs by Modern Artists, edited by George Sheringham and R. Boyd Morrison.

wore such hats all the time—while we were within the four-mile radius and out of doors. Only in August, and in the earlier weeks of September, did the average man dare to be seen wearing in the metropolis a hat of straw or felt. At other seasons, unless one were driving to a railway-terminus, with some luggage on the roof of the cab, such head-gear marked one out as something of an anarch. It seemed to be lacking in respect to Queen Victoria, though she herself was so seldom in our midst. When her son came to the throne, the top-hat began to totter upon our heads. He, after all, was a man: no question of chivalry was involved. Top-hats were rather heavy and hot. The heathen in their blindness bowed down to felt and straw. But they were conscious that this was not a right form of worship. Now they have lost altogether their decent misgivings. Nay, many of the younger ones worship nothing at all: they go about hatless, carrying high in the eyes of all beholders heads naked of aught but hair, without interference by the police. Oh for the less spacious times of great Victoria! But vain are the heart-cries of the fogey. The top-hat, so appropriate to the character of a London that is vanishing now—a London-ish, an unprovincialised and unamericanised London—is to all intents and purposes gone, extinct, hardly rememberable. The top-hat is never worn by anybody, except Ricketts. Not even by Shannon. And yet—I won't despair of Shannon. It is many years since he joined the Royal Academy, suddenly. And Ricketts was separable. He followed his friend only the other day. Perhaps I shall see Shannon in a top-hat yet.

I wonder, does Ricketts wear that collapsible crown of his only when he dines out? Or does he, when he comes home, close it with a quiet snap and place it under his pillow, ready for the first thing in the morning? Some painters wear hats when they are working, to shade their eyes. Does Ricketts at his easel wear his gibus? It would seem to me incongruous with his canvas. He is sensitively keen on many periods in the world's history; but I have never noted in his work any trace of absorption in the manners of Victoria's time: his mind ranges further back and wider afield. The rigid top-hat is at any rate a thing of the Regency; and so late as the eighteen-fifties any gentleman attending an evening party glided into the drawing-room with that hat in his left hand, and was not parted from it. The gibus is a mere mushroom. I would even call it a toadstool, for it is redolent of that sinister thing, the growth of machinery—our world's blight and curse. An ingenious little machine it is, I grant you. I can enjoy the plop and the snap of it myself. But its charm is not comparable with that of the top-hat proper. It can play its two tricks, but it has no moods. It cannot be rubbed the wrong way. It doesn't care how you treat it. And its nature is dull, sombre. It never comes radiant from the iron, flashing broadly back the single light of the sun, or narrowly back as many artificial lights as may be cast upon it; whereas—

But I cannot make the juvenile reader share my faded old enthusiasm. He derides me as a praiser of the pot at the expense of the kettle. His desire is for colour and for fantasy. That is very natural. In about 1830 there was inaugurated (for men only) a tyranny of black and white and grey, and of austere prosaicism in form. In about 1910 there was at last a slight and timid reaction. Socks and ties were often quite vivid, until, in 1914, the great tidal wave of khaki overwhelmed them. At the withdrawal of that they re-appeared, these details, and were welcomed. In 1925 there was, I perceived, even a touch of fantasy. The Oxford trousers and the "pull-over" were a step in the right direction; but a slight step and the only one. I applaud the young men's desire for fantasy and colour. I do but wish they would show more inclination to satisfy it. To all intents and purposes, the aspect of the streets of London is no more en-livened by men's costume than it was when first I knew it. Only on the stages of some theatres do fantasy and colour, for both sexes, abound and thrive.

[64]

True fantasy is a rather recent thing there. In panto-mimes and ballets there was always some fantasy, of course; but it was of a perfunctory and stale order. In Shakespearean and other "costume" plays there never was any stint of colour, and the colours were often lovely; but fantasy was barred, in costumes as in scenery. Gordon Craig started the revolt, designing costumes, as he designed scenery, rather from his inward fancy than by recourse to facts. The de-signing of theatrical clothes became a creative art. Ricketts, William Nicholson, Albert Rutherston, Dulac, Glyn Philpot, George Sheringham, Boyd Morrison, and other gifted men, have revelled in it. Of course, what the actors and actresses wear is not really quite so important as what they say and how they say it. A very dowdily-dressed performer, speak-ing lines that are worth hearing, and speaking them in such a way that they can be heard by people who have not ob-tained seats in the front row of the stalls, will achieve a greater success than can be hoped for by a divinely clad rival who does otherwise. Still this rival cuts a fine figure, and the hearts of the audience glow with gratitude to the designer of the wondrous effect. "And," says the audience to itself, "artists are notoriously vain and selfish. If this de-signer can thus glorify others, what must his own raiment be!" And at the fall of the curtain there arises a loud cry, "Designer! Designer!" The call is not taken. The cry per-sists, rising to a key of anger. The manager comes on, rather pale, to say that the designer is "not in the house." The manager, believe me, is a liar. The designer is there, right enough, but he dares not show himself. You ask me why he is so diffident? Really I haven't time to give a verbal ex-planation of a matter so subtle. I will do a drawing.

I have done the drawing. Dulac I had to omit, for it is ten years since I had the pleasure of meeting him, and he may have metamorphosed in the meantime. There was just a touch of romanticism in his costume (as there was also in that of the lamented Lovat Fraser), but the colouring was

[65]

sternly subdued: black and darkest grey were the notes. Glyn Philpot is not here, because I find his face very difficult to portray. As to his clothes, I assure you that no conclave of the soberest pundits of Savile Row would find one point in them for deprecation. I have given Ricketts the small sombrero that I had always associated with him. When one does a drawing, what is one glimpse as against the vision of a lifetime? I thought I might brighten the group by giving Nicholson a canary-coloured waistcoat. But sincerity forbade. It is many years since he ceased to strike that note of colour for us. Albert Rutherston eschewed, from the very outset of his career, aught that is conspicuous in hue or fashion. George Sheringham is equally discreet. So is Boyd Morrison. Craig at one time used to wear no necktie, but always wears one nowadays. Also, he wears the overcoat that you see here, in preference to his cloak. And was the cloak itself extraordinary, after all? Not really, when one comes to think of it. Painters and poets had been wearing such cloaks throughout the Victorian Era. The young gentlemen of the Quartier Latin were wearing them, as we all know, in the days of Gavarni. Why should mere sleevelessness be the symbol of revolt against the established order of things? Why don't our rebels invent new symbols, as they go on? A black cloak, with a black sombrero—surely this eternal formula cannot for ever satisfy the insurgent soul of youth and genius. In France it certainly doesn't. The students in Paris do ever run changeful riot in corduroy, velvet, and all manner of fabrics, dyed in all manner of colours. There is evidently some deep-rooted national difference— something that inhibits our rebels in their wish to look rebellious, and tones down to a timorous gloom the expression of their ardours. Even that brightness of ties and socks which quite conventional young men dare to indulge in is beyond their range. It is all very sad. What is to be done about it?

I appeal to the designers of theatrical costumes. Doubt-

less they have hoped that the orgies of colour and fantasy
with which they grace the theatres would have a marked
effect on the streets, instead of merely making the streets'
effect duller than ever by contrast. I suggest to these eminent friends of mine that they should design costumes not
merely for actors and actresses, but also for citizens. I hear
them murmur that there would be no demand for these, but
I am not deterred. Let them, I say, make the demand themselves. Let them go around setting the example. This is a
splendid idea. I am too excited to write about it. I will do
another drawing.

I have done the drawing. It rather disappoints me. But it
might be worse. I need hardly explain that the costumes are
entirely haphazard. I didn't attempt (I was too excited) to
do designs characteristic of the men drawn. I just clothed
them hurriedly in anything bright that occurred to me.
Only once did I pause. I was about to give Ricketts an opera
hat of many colours. But this would have been to carry
fantasy too far; and I curbed my foolish pencil.[1]

[1] These two drawings are now in the Birmingham City Museum and
Art Gallery. They are reproduced (alas, in black and white only) in *A
Catalogue of the Caricatures of Max Beerbohm* (1972).

Two Glimpses of Andrew Lang

THE FIRST OF these was in the summer of 1896, at an afternoon party given by Mr and Mrs Edmund Gosse at their house in Delamere Terrace. I think this was also the first time I was at that delightful house. My *Works* had just been published; and to Gosse, whom I had already met often enough, I had sent a copy. He was not quick to patronise young men who had done nothing, nor those who had done nothing good. Sidney Colvin would sit demurely benign, exquisitely trustful of the outcome, on any egg—on any number of eggs. Gosse cared but for the fledged and able-bodied chick. I remember that when I received my summons to Delamere Terrace I felt that my little book really had not fallen flat.

The drawing-room was very full when, carefully dressed for the part of brilliant young dandy, and very calm, and very shy, I made my entry. Mrs Gosse had been reading *The Works* and introduced me, as author of them, to some lady at hand. I stood talking to this lady about the weather, inwardly hoping that she was thinking how kind it was of me to talk down to her level, and that she was not guessing that I would have liked very much to dazzle her if I had known how. But while I talked, I thought less of the impression made by me on this lady than of the deep impression made on me by Mr Andrew Lang. I had instantly recognised him from the photographs. He was leaning against an angle of the wall. One might almost have supposed that he had been placed there as an ornament, like a palm in a pot. From the buzzing human throng he seemed to be quite as detached as any palm in any pot. Slender and supereminent, he curved, he drooped, he was a very beautiful thing in the room. And it was even more in colour than in form that he was so admirable. To think that Nature, and not some cunning handicraft of staining and bleaching, had produced these harmonious contrasts! The long nut-brown neck was not more sharply relieved by the white of the turned-down collar than was the nut-brown forehead by the silvery hair that wavily caressed it, than were the nut-brown cheeks by the silvery vapour they had of whisker. And the moustache was jet-black, and jet-black were the eyebrows and the eyelashes. In such surroundings the whiteness of the eyeballs and the darkness of the brown eyes "told" tremendously, of course. But in a spiritual sense the eyes told nothing at all. They shone, they flashed, but with no animation to belie the general look of inanimateness. Their lustre was as lovely and as meaningless as that of jewels. Nature had in some corner of the earth produced two large brown diamonds, of which she was very proud; and it had seemed to her that Andrew Lang's face would be the best of all possible settings for them. So there they were. I wondered whether, with things of such fabulous value exposed on his person, he went about armed, or unarmed but very heavily insured. Now and again, as he stood propped against the angle of the wall, he inserted with long brown fingers a monocle through which the rays of the eye were refracted with surpassing brilliance. And his manner of doing this seemed to indicate, not that there was any one whom he particularly cared to inspect, but that he took a languid pleasure in the gesture. If to superficial observers the fixing of that monocle might have convicted him of curiosity, the marked way he had of letting it drop promptly down again to his waistcoat must have acquitted him of having found the slightest profit in the investigation. With his white waistcoat he wore a pale blue tie. That was the note he had added to Nature's colour-scheme; and it was well chosen. It was good, too, as a symbol. It suggested just that detachment from Oxford which (since your thorough Oxford man is superior to everything, not excepting Oxford) stamped Andrew Lang as one of the most inalienably Oxfordish persons of his time.

Now that I saw him in person, I was loth to lose sight of him, but I did with a good grace escort my lady down to the dining-room, where were refreshments. When we came up again, Lang was no longer visible: the palm had been transplanted—whither?—and the corner where it had stood looked very bare. Presently my host came up to me and said, "Come out on the balcony. I want you to know Andrew Lang."

There he was, gazing across the balustrade to the canal whose nymphless waters, flow very near to Delamere Terrace.

"The angler aroused!" murmured Gosse. And "Yes," he said to Lang, in that tone of mock-lyric ecstasy which his friends know so well, "that is where I always go a-fishing, the first thing in the morning. Oh, you should breakfast with us! Trout, salmon, dace—I know not what! . . . But now I want you to know Mr Max Beerbohm, whose Collected Works have recently been issued."

"Yes, I've just been hw-eading them," Lang drawled in a tenor voice to Gosse. (To me he tendered a graceful hand, and his gaze wandered away.) "Ve-wy amusing," he faintly added.

"Why, Sir, I have read them and found neither amusement in their folly nor in their precocity the symptoms of salubrious growth" is what Dr Johnson would have said, and is what Lang conveyed. But those words might have been for me the beginning of a lifelong friendship with Dr Johnson, whereas Lang's "ve-wy amusing" was clearly a cul-de-sac.

And yet I daresay he meant to be kind. I have heard from people who knew him intimately that he was a really kind man. He may even have had the wish to please. But it is certain that one had to know him intimately before his wish could, in regard to oneself, be gratified. No man can easily be popular who has the Oxford manner in even a rudimentary degree: the perfection of that manner is a sovereign charm against popularity. (I have praised it in one of my books; but the eulogy was a trifle insincere—was a throwback to the time when I had not yet outgrown my undergraduate self. Oxford I have never ceased to love; but its manner—as exemplified not in writing, but in social intercourse—I began to abhor very soon after I went down.) It is no wonder that Lang was not beloved by people at large.

Especially was he not beloved by the eminent creative writers of his time. Indeed, very few critics get on well with creators. There is, no doubt, a point at which criticism does merge into creation, and it is always hard to say just where this point is—to determine whether this or that piece of fine criticism may or may not truly be called creative. But to this point, assuredly, Lang was never near. With all his gifts, he had of imagination not one spark. Fancy and wit he had in his earlier work; and grace he never lost; but for the rest he had only an immense quantity of that "cleverness" which to the creative artist is of all qualities the most repellent. And this cleverness, which was always at the disposal of the classics, was never used in service of any great contemporary writer. He helped Stevenson, because Stevenson was a Scotsman imitating Scott (instead of following the true bent of his own fantastic genius, alas). For Browning and Meredith and Swinburne, for Henry James, for Bernard Shaw, for any spirit that was new or vital in current work, he had at best a chilly tolerance. Himself remote by nature, he could enjoy masterpieces only at a distance: their proximity jarred him. He loved "Mr Thackeray," but he loved Jane Austen more: she was farther off. And Homer he loved most of all, because Homer was farther off than anyone. I think there was moreover in him (with his Gipsy blood) a strain of pure mischievousness that impelled him to poke fun at any great man who was alive to be annoyed. And this I take to be the reason why he would write now and again a sudden rhapsody about some obviously third-rate new talent. I remember dear old Theodore Watts-Dunton thumping the table in his back-dining-room and saying in his most sonorous accents, "I never yet knew a man of genius who didn't loathe Lang." He himself was the perfect type of the critic whom men of genius love. I am not a man of genius; but this did not prevent me from loving old Theodore. It did, however, prevent me from loathing Lang. I merely shared the common lot of men who met him for the first time: I did not like him.

Some years elapsed before I saw him for the second time. This was on a summer evening and in the courtyard of the Hotel Cecil. I had been invited to the annual dinner in aid of the Printers' Pension Fund. As I drove up, Lang was standing bare-headed on the steps, gazing brilliantly and blankly across the courtyard. He had not changed in the interval of years; the harmony of his silver and black and brown was all unimpaired. I don't suppose I had changed much either, but it never struck me that he would remember me. I was surprised when he held out that languid hand, with no sign that we had not parted from each other only a few hours before. I think I should have felt a little flattered, had not his manner seemed rather to imply that he had not taken the trouble to forget me. He said "These dinners are hw-ather a bore, aren't they?" "Well, they're not compulsory," I might have answered; but I never wanted to put an elder man—or, for that matter, a coæval or junior—at a disadvantage. Or again, I might have said truly that I myself always rather enjoyed any sort of public dinner, provided I was to be seen at the high table. But of course I did not make this confession of innocent vanity. I merely echoed Lang's opinion that these dinners were rather a bore.

At the meal I found myself next to Sidney Lee. It appeared that Lang and he and I (a strange triad) had been invited as representatives of Literature. Lang had been placed on the right-hand side of the Chairman—Mr Somebody M.P., an eminent Nonconformist (I was told) and, with his full black whiskers and prolonged shorn upper-lip and stout short body, a perfect type of British bourgeoisie, a marvellous foil to Lang. Lee and I were further along the table, and I had an uncomfortable feeling that Lee felt he ought at least to have been placed on the Chairman's left. This was not the first occasion on which I had sat next to him. I had been his guest at a dining-club— the Tatlers. I think he rather liked me, and that this senti- ment was on the whole sufficient consolation for his being, as it were, bracketed with me as representative of Literature. Certainly I liked him. He had for me the same sort of charm as had poor Churton Collins. One expected him to be dry and overbearing, as in his books he pre-eminently was, and to appal one with his erudition. One found a cheery, cosy, ruddy fellow, with a great zest for food and wine, a great capacity for receiving trivial gossip, and a great love of good cigars. My own appetite for food was always, to my regret, small. I loved the idea of a lot of it. The prospect of a very long dinner always kindled me. But in the actuality I was a weakling, unless, by good fortune, my neighbour were a tower of strength—in which case, by sheer force of ex- ample and of my own quick sympathies, I too could eat a great deal with much enjoyment and with no evil result. Even if on this particular evening I had been going to make a speech, I think my nervousness would not have prevented me from eating heartily.

After dinner, in one of the intervals between the toasts, Lang came and talked to us. He was presently to respond for Literature—a duty which he described as rather a bore. Lee, whose mind was more remarkable for massive grasp and sincerity than for quickness, agreed, through a puff of cigar-smoke, that it must be rather a bore. "For *you*," I said to Lang, implying that Lee and I and the other three or four hundred diners were looking forward to a great

[73]

treat. Lang smiled wearily, and said "The Chairman's a te-wible fellow. It seems he's a Member of Parliament or something of that sort," and wandered back to his place. To me the Chairman did not seem "a te-wible fellow" at all. In the two speeches already made by him he had quite won my heart. He seemed so simple and good and solid; and, sentiment aside, I judged him, despite his mutton-chop whiskers and his dropped h's, so very much more necessary to the national welfare than Lang or myself or—no, not than Sidney Lee. And Lang's gibe at the House of Commons seemed to me a silly relic of those 'seventies and 'eighties during which the younger literary gentlemen really thought that not to be a literary gentleman was to be something rather lamentable and absurd. Lang's gibe at poor Mr Somebody was not jarring only because it was pathetic. I wondered whether his speech would exasperate the audience or provoke their pity. I foresaw no other alternative.

Meanwhile our Chairman was on his legs, dealing inimitably with "Litrachur." He called it all sorts of names, the lodestar of youth, the solace of the busy man, the handmaiden of religion—I know not what. "And though," he wound up, "we cannot all 'ope to climb those dizzy 'ights which 'ave been scaled by Mr Randrew Lang, by (glance at notes) Mr Sidney Lee, and (glance at notes) by Mr Max Beerbohm (I dropped my head and faintly snorted in deference to Lee), yet in our 'umble way every one of us may" etc., etc.

Lang, received with cheers, made merciless fun of the Chairman, but the fun was so light and good that the cruelty really did not matter. His public manner was very much better than his private one. The necessity for talking out and up into the air, so as to be heard in a large dining-hall, greatly improved him—gave him somewhat that air of vitality and geniality of which his lack was so chastening elsewhere. He left the Chairman for dead, but the death, one felt, had been painless; and he proceeded to deplore the invention of printing. Printing had been the bane of letters. All the magic of Homer, of Chaucer, of the Hebrew Prophets, was directly traceable to this immunity from the fear of being printed. . . . The idea was worked out very wittily. Public speaking seemed to galvanise not merely Lang's manner, but also his mind: his speech was as delightful as one of those *causeries* or those leading-articles with which, many years before, he had made his name in journalism, and by virtue of which he had so long thriven, in journalism, on his name.

The audience—composed entirely of men who had to do with printing—did not laugh nor cheer, and evidently took Lang's speech as a wholly serious rebuke of their calling. But, not less evidently, there was no resentment—merely an awed hearing for the views of a personage. Lang went on to regret that such a trifler as himself had been deputed to respond instead of Mr Sidney Lee or Mr Max Beerbohm. He pronounced a great eulogy on Lee (to Lee's intense discomfort) and, if I remember rightly, spoke of the immense debt owed him by Shakespeare. The audience cheered respectfully. Then came a yet warmer panegyric of myself, with an elaborate parallel between me and Leonardo da Vinci—our passionate detachment from the follies and strifes of the outer world, our passionate devotion to the subtle labours we had set ourselves. Again the audience cheered, still quite respectfully. But the odd thing, as it seemed to me, was that I was inwardly pleased—almost as pleased as I should have been if Lang had paid me some tiny true compliment. To the really vain person (especially if he be also really modest) ironic praise is better than no praise at all. I remember my brother Herbert once said "I can stand any amount of flattery—if it's only fulsome enough". And I replied "Oh, *I* make no conditions of any sort".

Ever after that speech at the Hotel Cecil I felt more cordial towards Lang. Had I met him again in person, perhaps I should have been chilled. But I met him only in print. The place where I most frequently thus met him was the *Illustrated London News*. There he appeared, week by week, in circumstances that touched sharply one's sense of pathos. Week by week, there was Chesterton rolling and rollicking up and down the columns of the front page, reeling off ideas good, bad, and indifferent—but always ideas, and plenty of 'em, and plenty more where they came from. And there on one of the back pages was Andrew Lang also, his words interspersed by the Editor with numerous little photographs, of things in general—circular photographs, ovals, quadrangles, around which his words had to trickle as best they might. And the sad truth was that these words deserved no better treatment than they got—such tired words as they were about such trivial points in such tedious subjects of research: Did Angus MacNob wait for Prince Charlie at the back-door of the inn, as Professor Chittabob declares, and not at the side-door, as tradition has it? I wondered whether Lang himself cared about such things any more than the public which skipped what he had to say about them. Would Chesterton some day fall back on such things? Once upon a time Lang had been alive and alert as Chesterton. A terrible thing, Time. I wondered what Lang felt about Chesterton. What, in the fourth row of the ballet, while the vigorous prima ballerina pirouettes along the footlights, is felt by the faded and emaciated woman who in her day was prima ballerina? Perhaps she is merely glad she is still able to earn *something*. . . . I thought it likely that Lang, for his name's sake, was paid quite as much as Chesterton. Still, that he had to go drearily on, pointing in that public obscurity his superannuated toes, was an odious matter for reflection. When I learned, after his death, that he had left twelve thousand pounds, I was glad his need had not been so pressing as I had supposed—glad it was rather the force of habit that had kept him so constantly "at it." A terrible thing, Time, nevertheless.

[*Life and Letters*, June 1928]

A. B. Walkley

PUBLIC OPINION is a queer and mystic affair; and the most successful persons are they who can divine it and then utter it as their own. I am almost entirely without the happy instinct by which such divination can be made. But now and again I can faintly discern in the great dark sea of collective thought an exceptionally strong current; and during the past few years I have been aware of a feeling throughout the English-speaking world that it was high time for Mr Walkley to range himself (as he would say), to settle down. This feeling will be intensified by his latest book. *Pastiche and Prejudice* is the work of a man impenitently young.

What is to be done with him? I ask this with special venom because I too am a writer. Writing is an arduous business. If you do a little of it, by fits and starts, as the fancy takes you, then you can contrive to seem hardly older than you are. But the constant practitioner—how quickly he ages! Such a practitioner is Mr Walkley; yet time and custom try vainly to wither and stale him and to keep us thereby in countenance. He is monstrous. Many years ago, when I was an undergraduate, reading his weekly articles in the *Speaker* and his more frequent articles in the *Star*, his freshness and verdure did not anger me. I imagined him to be a very precocious man of about my own age. The high spirits that went with his wisdom, the sudden little out-bursts of sheer impudence that variegated his admirable *tenue*, gave me a sense that he and I were boys together. Later, I found that we were not coæval; and I was glad; whenever my elders blamed me for kicking up my heels, I directed their attention to the heels of Walkley. But in due

[77]

course, when I had begun to feel around my ankles the sobering clutch of the fingers of the years, I rejoiced at the news that he was henceforth to write unsigned dramatic criticisms for an old-established and very august newspaper. I thought this would sober even *him*. But no! Through the veil of the first-person-plural he was as evidently himself as ever—he and his heels. Two decades or so have passed; yet the strange performance is unabated; and so excellent is it that I should (jealousy aside) be glad to have in book-form all that is written for *The Times* anonymously, and on the spur of the midnight moment, by A.B.W. But he was ever fastidious, and he chooses to offer just a selection of those more leisured essays which he writes over his own (quite superfluous) initials.

Perhaps it was with some hope of becoming a writer congruous with his years that he recently began to compose *pastiches*. Addison and Henry James, Jane Austen and Anatole France—mightn't their styles, and the difficulty of imitating them, weigh him down a little and make him seem at any rate a trifle older than he spiritually is? One gathers that he approached his task in a rather solemn and sombre spirit. "Parody," he says, "is the pitfall of all *pastiche*." He regrets that M. Marcel Proust's versions of Balzac and Saint-Simon were "a little more like Balzac and Saint-Simon than the originals themselves." But surely that was a merit? What point would there have been in exact reproduction? M. Proust's motive was not that of Chatterton; and *pastiches* in general should be valued in so far as they are, through stress laid on salient characteristics of thought and manner, a criticism of their subjects. I will not lament with A.B.W. that his own exercises "never rise above parody"; for if they did so they would not be the acute and enlightening commentary that they are; and they would be dull instead of being, as they are, riotously funny. Never has A.B.W. given so strange a proof of his youthfulness as in these belated but triumphant excursions

[78]

into a field hitherto unfrequented save by striplings.

I wonder if he has really lost his "schoolboy enthusiasm over Macaulay's style." He says he has, but I doubt it. Not, of course, that he has anything in common with Macaulay—except the knack of being irresistible. Macaulay was ever a prejudiced writer, and A.B.W. has never appeared to dislike anything but dullness, pretentiousness, coarseness. The *and Prejudice* of his title is inappropriate, and must be taken as a mere vague gesture of homage to his adored Jane Austen. It is she and her like, the "delicate and formal" spirits in literature, that have always appealed to him most surely. And I have often wondered that the delicate formality of his own style can, even with the aid of the boyish gusto that underlies it and breaks through it, hold its own so well, in the midst of a great journal filled with news of yesterday's great events. I doubt (though he will be shocked) whether the adored Jane could hold her own in the circumstances with which he himself contends so successfully. He is stronger, mightier than Jane. But not to an extent that would be disastrous. For the most part, what is good in a newspaper is perfectly dreadful in a volume. Of A.B.W. it may truly be said that he is even better in a volume than in a newspaper. Collection is a great test. Things that seem good enough separately may be tedious in a gathering of them. But really good things help one another loyally. Every essay in *Pastiche and Prejudice* is the more delectable through its fellowship with the rest.

Most of them are on themes of drama or of literature, and are the work of a man who has always been intensely interested in "form." I would back A.B.W. against twenty pedants—if he could be bothered to play their game. But he can't. With all the canons and niceties that he has at his finger-tips, it is life that most enchants and amuses him. The confirmed Philistine need not fear that this book will bore him. But its fullest appeal will be to people who, having something of A.B.W.'s own keen scent for "form," can

[79]

appreciate the exquisite artfulness of construction that has gone to the making of every separate essay—the solidity and rotundity of all these single little works of art. Very light they seem. But the secret of that effect is in the perfection of the workmanship.

In one respect only do I detect signs that A.B.W. has aged since first I studied his work. He seems to have somewhat lost that air of detachment and disdainfulness which is so characteristic of youth. Charitable he always was, but not hearty: gay rather than genial. Dramatists and actors he regarded evidently as an uncouth race, and it did not seem that he ever descended into any personal relation with them. But now, behold him enshrining in his prose a remark made to him "by the late Henry Neville," and also quoting from a letter written to him by Sir Arthur Pinero. Stranger still and even more significant is the avowal of a melting mood. He says that there are in *Caste* scenes that he cannot read "without tears." . . . Am I sorry or glad? I am not sure. Do I rejoice in the general juvenility of A.B.W. more than I resent it, or less? I do not know.

[*The Times*, 15 September 1931]

A Sight that Gladdened Me

"WOULDN'T YOU like to stop and see your old rooms?" The question was put to me at about 1 p.m., on a wintry day, and on Magdalen Bridge, three years ago, by a friend who was motoring me from London to have luncheon with people in a house not far beyond Oxford. You will have inferred that the friend was not Philip Guedalla, who, in the first number of this Magazine, told you that "the return to Oxford starts at the railway-station," and gave beautifully cogent reasons for that doctrine. I yield to no one in hatred of motor-cars as a general institution. Who but a not very precocious child would? They have done more for the ruin of civilization than any other kind of machinery that has us in its grip. Aeroplanes will presently have outstripped them in this line, no doubt. But meanwhile the palm is to the motor-cars. And yet—and yet—in this one little (or rather, great) matter of the return to Oxford, I venture, diffidently but firmly, to dissent from Philip. He is ever so much younger than I, and when first he went up to Oxford motor-cars were already coming to the fore, and railway-trains and their stations had taken on for him a tinge of romance. Even I can perceive that tinge; but it's a dingy tinge, after all. It's a tinge of an old incipient barbarism, of a horror less horrid only than the horrors that were in store. And no grace of romance had it possessed in 1890, the date of my own up-coming. I was glad that Oxford had with a finely arrogant and repellent gesture put the railway-station so far away from her. But I regretted that she hadn't shoo'd the thing still farther away; and ever after I used the thing sullenly, as a makeshift for what should be.

[81]

By coach, or on horseback, or in a gig, or even in a carrier's cart, or (heaven help one!) on foot, seemed to me the proper way of entry into the matchless town. And when, long after, in the reign of King Edward, and in the bloom of my early middle age, one of the queer new machines took me across Magdalen Bridge and left me at The Mitre, I felt that my coming had at last *something* of the old right manner about it.

So did I feel again three years ago, after a lapse of more than twenty years in which I had not seen Oxford. But I had other feelings too, of a finer and more impersonal kind. And thus when the intuitive Bengal Lancer suddenly asked me the question that I have here recorded, I was slightly hurt. It was as though he had said, "Aren't you rather an egoist?" But all the egoist in me fervently answered, "Yes, I should." Yeats-Brown flashed his monocle on to his wristwatch. There were five minutes to spare.

We swerved down Oriel Street, we alighted at Merton. I had dwelt in Mob Quad ("the oldest quadrangle in Oxford," I impressed upon Yeats-Brown), on the ground-floor, under the Library, my windows commanding an unbeloved view of the New Buildings that line one side of a quadrangle that is nearer to the meadows. Lord Randolph Churchill, idol of all schoolboys in the 'eighties, had occupied my rooms in the late 'sixties and had carved his name large on a small side-table. Deeply was my young heart thrilled when my scout, ushering me in, displayed to me that signature. And now I would thrill Yeats-Brown with it—though perhaps he would only say, "Oh, yes. Winston's father. Fancy!" As a matter of fact he said nothing about it. He didn't see it. He didn't enter the room. The oak was sported. I knocked loudly—and wonderingly: in my day we didn't sport oaks at luncheon-time. "Perhaps the hermit is deaf; perhaps," I said, "we could catch a glimpse of him through my windows." We passed along to the outer quadrangle. There I caught sight of something that I thought was an illusion. I ignored it, turning to the matter in hand. Through my windows we saw nothing but window-curtains. A youth came strolling by. "Excuse me, sir, but"—I explained that I had once lived in these rooms, and had hoped to see them again. "I'm sorry, sir, but"—he explained that they were now an extension of the Junior Common Room, and were at present closed for some reason which I don't remember. I thanked him, sir, and turned to face boldly the illusion that had disquieted me. I became quite sure that it was something real, after all. I was much relieved, but not less bewildered. A miracle had been performed. When? By whom? How?

How came it that the New Buildings were new no more? —that the hideous smug towering structure by Butterfield towered no longer? and had become beautiful? If three or four stories had been added aloft, and shops opened along the ground-floor, and the whole façade embedded in white concrete, I should have said, "Well, Merton is keeping pace with the times." Almost every aspect that I had loved in London was wrecked already by intrusion of things utterly out of scale; crude, dull, huge, blank, unimaginative, would-be-American erections; dismal and monstrous robot-warrens (a few of which, I was told, were not, despite these hard times, in very bad financial straits). And in *The Times* there had been a correspondence about some proposed new buildings in Oxford, and an eminent modernistic architect had coyly said that "one should not be afraid of the word sky-scraper" even in Oxford. Evidently he hadn't emboldened Merton. Merton had timorously, gloriously, knocked off the whole of Butterfield's top story, and had hidden the rest of his work, transforming it with stone which tallied with that of the elder buildings. Merton was no longer dwarfed and contradicted by Butterfield. She was her own dignified little mediæval self once more. She had set a very strange example. I felt very proud of her.

I should have liked to linger with her and feast my eyes on

the view of the meadows through the fine iron gateway with which she had graced the old blank wall. But I was sure she would not wish Yeats-Brown and me to arrive late for luncheon. Away we hurried, he glad of the pleasure he had given me, and I with an incipient feeling that I, as a Merton man, was partly responsible for Merton's great act. I hadn't exactly prompted it, of course, but—

At any rate the prompter, and generous abetter, was an old friend of mine; a coæval of mine at Merton and my earliest friend there. I didn't boast of this to Yeats-Brown, for I was unaware of the fact. It was some weeks later, in Italy, that the fact was casually revealed to me. I heard it with emotion. The years and the seas have parted Albert Burney and me. But across them I send him my love and deep respect.

[*Oxford*, Winter 1934]

My Ambitions

EVER REMEMBER, my dear Dan, that you should look forward to being some day manager of that concern."

These words, in the eighteen-sixties, made a great impression on the mind of Mr Matthew Arnold. He had read them in a report of a speech made by Sir Daniel Gooch, a well-known industrial magnate. The young Daniel, when he was little more than an infant, had been employed in the great iron foundry near which his parents lived in very humble circumstances. But the heart of his mother had not been humble, in regard to him; and she had often, pointing a finger at the dominant and fuliginous building, spoken to him the words that I have quoted. To these he attributed, in great measure, his signal success in life; he had been as much impressed by them as was, in later years, Mr Arnold, who, in one of the essays in *Culture and Anarchy*, cited them not once but (in that lingering and loving way of his) many times, and called them "Mrs Gooch's Golden Rule." Alas, this description must not be taken at its face value. Some twenty years ago Mrs Humphry Ward, in a public rebuke of Lytton Strachey, said that irony was "always a coward's weapon." If her aphorism was just, her uncle was one of the most abject cowards of the previous century. It is true that whenever he wrote poetry he was brave and straightforward enough in expression of his strange dislike for the great industrial days in which he lived. Such lines as

> *this strange disease of modern life,*
> *With its sick hurry, its divided aims,*
> *Its heads o'ertaxed, its palsied hearts,*

[85]

are, much as they were resented, and may still be resented, pardonable by reason of their pluck and their simplicity. But whenever he descended to the plains of prose he lost his nerve and became horribly nimble with the coward's weapon—plying it with dastardly skill not only against the great industrialists, but also against the most eminent leaders of the Nonconformist Churches, and the most popular believers in the divine wisdom of representative assemblies, and the most acclaimed heralds of the imminence of a bland smug general perfection. It would seem that Mr Arnold disliked successful men. Early in the eighteen-eighties, at a banquet holden in Balliol, with the Master (that very successful man, Dr Jowett) presiding, and with a galaxy of Proconsuls, Bishops, Cabinet Ministers, Judges of the High Court, and divers other luminaries who had been alumni of that College, Mr Arnold, in responding to the final toast, the toast of Literature, claimed that in such a symposium he might not be unwelcome as one who had been quite frankly a failure in life. Well, it is true that his writings had brought him no more than a pittance, and that he had still to earn his living by travelling around the counties as an Inspector of Schools, asking little boys and girls to give the date of the Battle of Agincourt, and to name the capital of Turkey. But, as there is no English writer whose poetry *and* prose together give me so much pleasure as his, I can't agree that he had wholly failed. Perhaps he himself, behind his stiff Victorian shirtfront, didn't *really* believe that he had done so. One never knows where one is with these ironists.

It is, of course, conjecturable that his mother had often said to him, pointing towards the peak of Parnassus, "Ever remember, my dear Matt, that you should look forward to being some day manager of that concern," and that in his later years he genuinely wished he were the man whom the public regarded as manager of it, Lord Tennyson. But this is a flimsy hypothesis. I'm pretty sure Mrs Arnold had said nothing of the sort to her dear Matt—nor Mrs Tennyson to her dear Alf. Mothers are very percipient; and each of these two ladies may have thought her son likely to be a poet, and have hoped he would be a very good one . . . but the best one? or the most successful one? no! she wouldn't have bothered about that. She would have felt there was something rather cheap in that idea of competition, that fond dream of devil-take-the-hindmost and God-anoint-the-foremost. Even Mrs Gooch, had there been an Heliconian glint in little Dan's blue eyes, might have said, "Ever remember to write nicely, and don't worry your little head about anything else."

But there was no such glint; and all, from the commercial standpoint, was well. And all, from that standpoint, may, for aught I know, be well in a case of which I was told some years ago (and when a man so old as I says "some" he means many) by an eminent French sculptor. He had recently been commissioned to model a bust of a little boy aged seven, only child of an immensely rich father—a *"pharma-cien grandiose"* (exploiter of patent medicines)—and of a beautiful young mother, who was an ardent patron of the fine arts, but even more ardent adorer of *le petit* Marcel. The sculptor did not altogether share the maternal enthusiasm. Marcel was a restless and rather sullen sitter; and his beautiful little face never lit up in childish response to any efforts to make it do so. Fairy-stories were told, and little jokes made, in vain. From the time when his nurse brought him, to the time when his mother came to take him away, Marcel lacked animation; and the bust did not promise well. One day he was hopefully asked "What would you like to be when you are a grown-up man?" He gave no answer. "A soldier?" A shake of the head. "A sailor?" Another shake. "A chauffeur? A flying man? A farmer with cows and sheep? A sculptor like me?" Other shakes. "Then what, *mon cher petit bonhomme, would* you like to be?" "*Pharmacien.*" "*Ah, comme papa?*" The child answered in a toneless little voice, "*Plus riche que papa.*" When the mother arrived in due course, the sculptor told her smilingly this little piece of conversation; and she smiled too, saying, "I know better than he does. You have but to look at him! *Son avenir est déjà fixe. Il sera poète.*" But Marcel's words had impressed the sculptor less lightly, had for him indeed given to the child's face the significance, the soul, that had not seemed to be there. There it was; and the task was now both interesting and easy for my friend. But he was destined to look back on it with some regret. He had not, at any time, of course, shown to the mother the unfinished clay, and on this clay he still worked a little when no more sittings were needed. As soon as it had dried, he sent it round to the great house in the Champs Elysées, so that it should be approved before the casting of it in bronze. Next day Madame——came to the studio, pale and rigid, tragic. "Madame, what has happened? Tell me, I beseech you!" Silence. "Speak, Madame! Has the bust been dropped, broken? If so, no matter. I can do another—easily." Silence. "Your husband does not like it perhaps?" She spoke at last. "He likes it greatly, Monsieur. And it is not broken. But my heart is."

Here, you see, was a mother who became percipient only through a work of art. As aesthetes are very apt to exaggerate their emotions, we may reasonably hope that her heart was not really broken. Let us hope also that the father lived to rejoice in a son even more gloriously successful than himself. It was said by a wise man (by whom, I forget; so I say, as is usual on such occasions, by a wise man) that if one desires a thing strongly enough one is sure to attain it.

I remember that I once mentioned this saying to a well-known commercial magnoperator, and asked him whether he believed it true. He replied, "Yes; one gets just what one wants if one wants it with all one's heart and all one's soul." "And then?" I asked, with a slight sneer. "Oh, then," he said, "of course one finds one doesn't care a damn about it," and I deplored the tone of my question. But (like Madame ——) perhaps he exaggerated.

I hope so. *Palma non sine pulvere.* Dreadful to be half-choked with dust, and not to be proud of the palm! Lord Rosebery's tutor at Eton reported that he desired the palm without the dust; and dustlessly, in due time, was the palm handed to him. It is said that in his undergraduate days he told a friend that he meant to do three things: marry a Rothschild, win the Derby, and become Prime Minister. Dustlessly he did so. But he was not accounted happy in his later years. It would seem that there is a catch somewhere in any kind of satisfied ambition. Are the thwarted strivers happier in the long run? Mr Monckton-Milnes, the Lord Houghton of later years, had great political ambitions. In the spring of 1880 a young gentleman, with a letter of introduction, called on the venerable Lord Beaconsfield, who had long ago dropped the habit of saying much. To make conversation, the young man mentioned that he had been breakfasting with Lord Houghton, and said how astonishingly young Lord Houghton seemed. "The disappointed," said Lord Beaconsfield, in his deep hollow voice, "are always young." A surprising remark, certainly. And, now that the world has been going on so long, remarks that surprise are usually unsound. But if you think this one over, and pass in review those of your elder friends or acquaintances who have had great ambitions unfulfilled, you will, I think, be impressed by the deep truth of it.

And . . . but you are growing impatient. What about *My* Ambitions? To this sharp inquiry I can only reply, with bowed head, that I never had any. I had merely some modest wishes—to make good use of such little talents as I had, to lead a pleasant life, to do no harm, to pass muster. And, with head still bowed, I agree with you that I ought not to have granted the Editor's very kind request that I should initiate this series of articles.

[*John O'London's Weekly*, 15 March 1940]

Last and Best[1]

T IS A HUNDRED years (or so) since I reviewed a book; and the Editor of the *Spectator*, very kindly wishing me to celebrate this centenary, has sent me attractive material for the celebration. Too attractive, in a sense. In my salad days I was fairly good at slating a book, but was dull in praising one, and now am likely to be duller still. I pause, wondering, "Couldn't I possibly slate this one?" Alas, no. I was always honest, even when young, and am now too old to turn over a new leaf. With a heavy heart I embark on eulogy.

The book is one that makes me wish I had known the writer much better than I did. I knew him for many years, and we had many friends in common, but I think we were not personally much interested in each other's doings. I had read *Dodo*, of course, when it burst upon the world, and thought it very brilliant—as, indeed, in a rather garish way, it was. And *The Babe, B.A.*, was a very bright affair also. But nobody pressed me to read the rather more serious novels that followed, year after year, though they too were very popular. Two or three of them I did read. Very bright they seemed to me, but thin, not very real. And now I find that Benson himself, in later years, felt as I did about them. "They lacked," he says, "the red corpuscle. . . . I had often tried to conceal my own lack of emotion in situations that were intended to be moving, by daubing them over with sentimentality." He excepts three or four works from this candid indictment, "but," he says, "I had lost or was fast losing any claims to be called a serious novelist," and

[1] A review of *Final Edition* by E. F. Benson, published in the *Spectator*, 1 November 1940. E. F. B. had died in February.

[90]

the spirit moved him to roam away into fresh fields of labour. He does not claim to have made in them any important discovery. Nevertheless he made one. He found himself.

He found also Charlotte Brontë. His book about her (the first of his biographical books) was an admirable study of character and circumstance. It was what we reviewers call "penetrating." It was tenderly acute and, with all due deference to the foregoing Mrs Gaskell, inflexibly judicial. In fiction he had been hampered by lack of power to create significant men and women. But here, created already *for* him, was Charlotte, and here Emily and those others; and his keen intelligence could work freely, at ease; and his innate gift for narrative shone as never before. He then strode, briskly, firmly, from Haworth Parsonage to Balmoral, where he abode with equally good results: his Victoria rivalled his Charlotte. And presently he gave us those two fascinating works, *As We Were* and *As We Are*, the ripe fruits of social experience and observation—the wisdom of a man in love with things past, and in charitable touch with present things. There was plenty of autobiography mixed in with those musings. And now, in *Final Edition* (the best, I think, of all his books), there is no lack of pensive digressions in what is mainly the story of Benson's own life.

For autobiography there is a huge demand nowadays, and a not less huge supply. But many of the autobiographists are, alas, gravely handicapped. They have not had interesting lives, or haven't very good memories, or aren't in themselves obviously interesting or charming persons, or haven't a gift for writing. Some of them, indeed, have all these handicaps, and so their perseverance is all the more creditable to them. It is not for doggedness that Benson can be extolled. He had not had to wrestle with any of those awful drawbacks. He had lived in the centre of things, he had a keenly discriminating eye, he knew intimately many people well worth knowing, he had a very clear memory for anything that mattered, anything characteristic or illuminating or amusing; and he could write: he had become, in course of time, master of a lucid, concise, light, flexible prose that exactly fulfilled his purposes; a prose abundant in natural felicities; a prose greatly superior to that of either of his brothers, who never were able to curb or chasten their immense facility. I remember a rather wicked fable told to me by a friend of the three. When Arthur lay dying, he still wrote continuously. Hugh and Fred had been sent for, Arthur was well-pleased to see them, but soon the fountain pen was travelling fast across the writing-pad. Hugh and Fred sat down, produced their own pads and pens, and resumed their work. Presently the nurse approached them, and said, in a low voice, "Your brother's heart has ceased to beat. But—it is very strange—he is still writing." "Strange? Not at all," said the brothers, and went on writing. As a matter of fact, of course, the three were very fond of one another, though none of them ever was able to admire the works of the other two. One of the most amusing scenes in *Final Edition* is that in which the three sit reading to their mother, one evening, at Tremans, caustic burlesques of one another's works. Each of the parodied was rather puzzled than pained, angrier than hurt. But "Oh, you clever people," said Mrs Benson, "why don't you all for the future write each other's books instead of your own? You do it so much better."

But amidst all the fun that pervades this book, one is conscious of a serious, a gallant and even noble character. E. F. Benson, unlike his respectively academic and ecclesiastic brothers, had always been a man of the world, a lover of society, and of various sports, and of travel. Twenty years ago he began to have symptoms of arthritis. Gradually he was crippled, but in the fell process he never lost heart, and he writes of it with complete stoicism—and even with blithe wit. Only once does he repine—and then, I am bound to say, without good reason. "The presence of him who shuffles along on a stick, and who cannot pick it up if he drops it, does not promote gaiety. . . . He may feel, among many faces and the alert movements of acquaintances, that he is a tiny speck of tarnish on their silver hours, and will wonder if they are not suffering him rather than welcoming." The last time I met him was at a luncheon party given not long ago by an old friend of ours. Of course one couldn't help feeling sorry for him. But how could one not have delighted in his talk, of which the sparkle was as gay, and the point as keen, as ever?

Then and Now

BY VERA LADY ELDERTON

ES, I shall be a hundred years old tomorrow morning—at 4.15, to be exact. And I think it was a very good idea of the Editor's to invite me to write a few words about the many changes that I must have seen in the course of a long life. Long, but not nearly long enough for *me*! I am not (but, thank Heaven, I feel as though I were) as young as ever I was; and to all intents and purposes, I *am*.

My earliest memory is of a summer's day when I was still an infant in arms. Mamma was dandling me up and down in the air, when in came Papa. I can see him now, flushed and with shining eyes, wearing his Garter star and riband, and can hear the exact tone in which he cried out, "By God, she has the prettiest little voice I ever heard!" Who "she" was I did not know till I was older. Papa had just come back from Kensington Palace, after hearing the speech delivered to her Privy Council by the young Queen Victoria.

Our town house was in Grosvenor Square, which I re-member as being in those days a rather dismal place. I thank Heaven that I am and shall always be abreast of the times. The great tall buildings are a great improvement, in my humble but animated opinion. Indeed, the whole of Mayfair has changed for the better. In my young days there was still a turnpike at each end of every street there, as a protection against the highwaymen who still abounded. These ramshackle old barriers did not, however, keep the bears away in wintry weather (and weather in those days could be far wintrier than it can now). The bears used to come down, maddened with hunger, from Hampstead and from Campden Hill, seeking whom they might devour. All doors had to be bolted at sunset. I remember how night after night in "the hungry 'forties" Papa would sit, loaded for bear, at the open window of the dining-room and account for many of these marauders. He left me his London game-book in his will, and I always wish I hadn't mislaid it. For he was one of the crack shots of his day.

Public executions must already, I think, have been abolished; for I certainly never saw one. But the famous Tyburn gibbet still reared its great height just where the eastern end of Connaught Place is now; and I remember that I once dared my twin-brother Henry to climb it—which he did, for he was a plucky and agile little rascal. One morning soon after that exploit, he dared me, *en revanche*, to sweep the main chimney of our house. I was rather daunted at first, but, to cut a long story short, I did in due course triumphantly wave my broom from the chimney-pot and scramble down again, black but proud. It so happened that Mr Charles Lamb, now famous as "the gentle Elia," dined at our house that evening (for Papa and Mamma, though they had not, I think, much in common, were both of them very fond of hearing puns made). Having recently written an article about chimneysweeps, Mr Lamb was much excited at hearing of my deed, and when I came down to dessert he said, "You ought to be a good card-player, for you follow *soot*," and I remember wondering rather, until the joke was explained to me, why every one laughed so much at what had been said by this gentleman. I can see him now —a short, thick-set man with a humorous twinkle.

Children in those days were, I think, more at liberty to go their own way than they are now. I don't know whether this was a good thing. I am inclined to think it must have been a bad one, so firmly do I believe in what is called "the latest." But the fact does, I think, remain that we Early-Victorian kiddies (or kids, as we were then less fondly called) enjoyed a larger latitude in climbing, etc, than our successors in the

[95]

next, the present, the better century. And perhaps the reason was that we were so vastly in the majority. What were a father and mother against twelve children? Families of twelve were *de rigueur* in those days. My parents' family numbered upwards of twenty, so that many of us knew each other only by sight, as it were. But even so there was, I think, more *camaraderie* among us than there is in the modern family of one or at most two.

On great occasions there would be a full muster of us, young and old. For instance, the whole tribe attended the opening of the Crystal Palace in '51, and I remember that during the ceremony I said in a shrill voice, "I'd like to smash all this glass!" But Papa, who was a friend of Sir Joseph Paxton, said *"Sh!"* and I quieted down—which was unlike me. If there had been some stones handy, things might have been different. I am always proud of the part I played in the Suffragette disturbances that occurred not so very long ago. But to return to earlier days. The funeral of the Duke of Wellington was a great event in our lives. The victor of Waterloo—"the Iron Duke," as he was called because of the iron shutters that he had put up at Apsley House when the mob broke his windows at the time of his opposition to the first Franchise Bill—had a great hold on the public imagination, and on ours especially, because as a young man he had made a proposal of marriage to Mamma, and had always remained, I think, rather *épris*. He often used to call on her, always with a bouquet of pink and white roses. I can see him now—a tall man with a cocked hat and rather a Jewish nose. I wish he could have lived long enough to lead the Balaclava Charge with Lord Cardigan, for indeed he was young to the last, and I am old-fashioned enough not to be able to write of him without emotion—at the risk of being (very rightly) sneered at by those gay young "intellectuals" with whom I get along so well.

Mention of Balaclava reminds me of the great night when news reached us of the fall of Sebastopol. That was "some-

thing like" a night! But it was destined to pale beside the
night when we heard of the relief of Mafeking, many years
later. My dear husband and I had dined at home that evening, and I remember we were having a violent quarrel about
something or other when in rushed our young friend Mr
Rudyard Kipling, waving a small Union Jack. He sank down,
breathless, on to a chair, and then, "Mafeking," he said, "is
relieved!" A few minutes later the three of us were dancing
arm in arm up and down Piccadilly, and round and round
Trafalgar Square, three among many millions of revellers
like ourselves, but next morning Kipling wrote his well-
known poem "Recessional." This was considered rather a
sudden volte-face by some of his friends. But genius cannot
be judged by ordinary standards. "Rudkip," as we all called
him, was certainly a man of genius. I often regret that he
never went into the House of Commons, for I think he would
have had a success there, being so interested in politics.

Of the older school of politicians, I think the famous
"Dizzy" was the one whose company I liked best. He had a
wonderful way of coining phrases. I was once privileged to
hear from his lips a pronouncement that became historic.
This was at one of Lord Houghton's famous breakfast parties
in Charles Street. The aged Premier had arrived in London
late on the previous night from the Congress of Berlin. Lord
H, as we sat down to table, inquired, "What was the upshot
of it all?" After a pause, Dizzy replied in his deep, hollow
voice, "I have brought back Peace, Retrenchment and Re-
form." The effect was electrical; and there ensued a long
silence, in which one could have heard a pin drop, before the
conversation became general. Mr Whistler, that very clever
American painter and wit, was among the guests, and so was
his rival Oscar Wilde, and I think the following anecdote has
never found its way into print. Whistler said something
more than usually witty. "Good heavens," said Wilde, "I
wish I had said that!" Whistler, quick as lightning, replied,
"Well, Oscar, I have noticed in the course of years that you

do not always avoid the vice of plagiarism, and I think it not unlikely that sooner or later you will repeat what I have just said, leaving your hearers to suppose that you, not I, originated it!" After the roars of laughter had subsided, Mr Alec Yorke (who was a Groom-in-Waiting) said, "I must tell that to the Queen." A few weeks later he told me that he had done so, and that the Queen had said that she was not amused; but it must be remembered that she was still in deep mourning for the Prince Consort, whom, by the way, I never met, for he "went out" very little, except in the circles frequented by "Candle" Faraday, "Evolution" Huxley, and others of the scientific persuasion. Not that I have anything to say against science. I regard it as an immense blessing and improvement in every way.

And now I must break off, for I have so much to do at the Cabaret-Canteen that I am running. But what I have written is not all that I shall write. I see no reason why I should not in the course of nature live to be two hundred, and I shall then offer to generations yet unborn many spicy memorials of the years to come.

[*Spectator*, 22 November 1940]

Remembered Meals[1]

N THESE DAYS of food-restrictions, I often let my memory rove back to meals that I especially enjoyed *dans le temps*. I use these three French words because it is mostly to France that these fond expeditions are made. More perhaps than anywhere else in France does my memory rejoice *chez* Voisin—Voisin the small, the serious, the old, the deeply dignified temple of gastronomy in which I was sometimes privileged to worship in my youth. Perhaps the Maison d'Or and the Café Anglais were as perfect as Voisin; but these two had vanished just before my day.

I am thankful that my day dawned a goodish while before Paris ceased to be exclusively Parisian—before she, in the goodness of her heart, built cocktail-bars for the Americans, beer-saloons for the Germans, tea-rooms for us, and great big restaurants with plenty of music in them for everybody. Voisin, few-tabled Voisin, had catered, decade after decade, for a few serious Parisians, learned in the art of eating and drinking, and for a few equally erudite members of the Corps Diplomatique. I always felt myself to be an intruder among those time-worn banquettes of green velvet fringed with faded gold lace; an intruder in the presence of those priest-like waiters, and of that sommelier whose manners were Archiepiscopal. But oh, how reverent an intruder!—and with an appetite whetted by spiritual exaltation.

When my memory is faithless to Voisin, it flits lightly to another, a very different, an unsophisticated place; a place in the open air; an orchard at Arques-la-Bataille. In the month

[1] First published in the *Abinger Chronicle*, Sept–Oct 1942. Revised and enlarged for the *Sunday Times*, 26 December 1954.

of August I went always to stay for a while at Dieppe. One
of the charms of that dear old town was that Jacques Blanche
lived near to it, at Offranville, delighting one with his wit
and with his omniscience and with his pathetic delusion that
he could learn from one something that he did not already
know.

Another charm was that Arques was within easy driving
distance. On fine mornings "Let's lunch at Arques" were
words very apt to spring to English lips; and anon a fiacre
was hailed, and one drove away, and presently passed the
great battle-field that looked so pacific in the sunshine, and
in due course one was welcomed by the inn-keeper and his
wife, and chose a table under one of the apple-trees and near
to the trout-stream that bordered one side of the orchard.

Fresh, ever so fresh from that stream came the first course
of the meal that one ordered. The table that one sat at did
not perhaps stand very straight, so uneven was the orchard's
ground. But it was a good solid kitchen-table, and the chairs
were of the same honest nature. The table-cloth and the
napkins were coarse, but of snowy whiteness; and I think
one liked them all the better for being still slightly damp
from the wash. The long rank grass was constantly patrolled
by a great number of hens, by an almost equally great number of cats, and by several large dogs—all of these creatures
taking a friendly but not unselfish interest in one. Their
appetite sharpened by its example one's own.

But even without their aid I should have been greedy
enough. Good food is peculiarly attractive in the open air. It
tastes better, purer than in any room, however well-
ventilated; and one wants more of it. The sight of something
in constant quick motion is also a sure appetiser. Years ago I
used to wonder why I always felt so hungry in a railway-
train and so avid of the luncheon-basket. I deduced that the
reason for this was the stimulating sight of the landscape at
full speed. And I am convinced that at Arques my notable
capacity for trout, for *poulet-en-casserole*, for *omelette-au-*

jambon, for Camembert or Brie, was in great measure due to the briskly flowing, the indefatigable little trout-stream at my side.

But away with scientific analysis! It is an outrage on memory. Let me but mention an Arquean meal that I recall with special clearness. There were four of us. The host was a friend of mine, well-known in London as a devotee of music and patron of musicians, well-loved for his kindness of heart and immense sense of fun. One of the guests was a life-long friend of his, a not greatly-gifted painter but a very good fellow and accomplished man of the world. Another was a beautiful young lady, full of intelligence and high spirits.

The sun shone fiercely on the orchard, but was tempered by a lively western breeze. The leaves of the tree above us were ever astir. Shifting dots of sunshine dappled the table-cloth and sparkled on the good red wine in the thick rustic glasses. We ate and ate, we laughed and laughed, long and long. The dogs, the cats, the hens looked up at us and marvelled at our gaiety. And the stream babbled with us. And all the world was young—seventeen years old perhaps, not more.

Rapallo Re-Echoes[1]

Y DEAR JAMES, The Editor of the *Manchester Guardian* has very kindly sent me a copy of *London Echoing*, and, very kindly too, invites me to review it. But it is so many long years since I reviewed a book that I have utterly forgotten how to perform that task presentably. Therefore I am merely writing a letter to you—and shall post it not to you, but to the Editor, asking him (though even Editors ought not to read private letters addressed to other people) to glance through it and, without showing it to you, publish it if he thinks it would pass muster in print.

Far be it from me to gush, even in strict privacy; but measured terms are not those in which I can express my gratitude to you for this sequel to *The London Perambulator* of 1925—a book that I have read and re-read many times and have never tired of. The splendid pictures by the great Muirhead, your brother, would have cast into the shade any writing that wasn't splendid too. And now here you and he are again, to enthral me jointly. You object that to your way of writing the epithet "splendid" isn't applicable? I agree. I remember that when I was quite a small boy I was taken to hear a lecture given by a very orotund old Irish barrister on "The English Humourists." As an instance of Charles Lamb's felicity in choice of words, he quoted, with deep unction, "the dusty splendour of St Paul's." Then he paused. "Splendid? It is not splendid. Dusty?—The notion's absurd. But," with upcast eyes, "DUSTY SPLENDOUR-R!" And you, James, remind me of St Paul's. Your splendour is

[1] A review of *London Echoing* by James Bone, published in the *Manchester Guardian*, 18 September 1948.

dusty. So was Charles Lamb's. You remind me of him, too. You are always happiest when your beams of light are filled with the motes of the dust of old things vanished. You're a wondrous rememberer, as was Elia: a most warm and cosy recorder of things scythed away by that brute, Saturn. You object to the word "brute"? No doubt. Like Elia, you are inveterately Gentle. You never rail at the present, at science and mechanism and vandalism and uniformity and insipidity and so on, as do I and so many others. You are best pleased to write of what you have loved—queer old shops, queer old taverns; queer old shopmen and inn-keepers: "odd fish," as Elia called the old clerks at the South-Sea House, and the old Benchers of the Inner Temple.

Again you object?—pointing out (gently) that during the greater part of your life you have been a Fleet Street man, ever alert in a maelstrom of current events. You have indeed. And nothing could be more vividly "actual" than (for instance) your account of the crowd outside Buckingham Palace when Edward VII was dying, or your notation of the difference in the public emotion at the close of the first European war from its emotion at the close of the second one. But even in times of intensest stress you are not forgetful of arcane corners. I remember lunching with you in Soho on the day of Neville Chamberlain's second flight to Germany and how much you disheartened me with "inside information" that nothing would come of it, forasmuch as Hitler was in the worst of moods. But after the meal you atoned by giving me a great treat: you took me round to a strange old low-ceilinged shop which, in an adjacent street, had been kept by the members of one family for more than a hundred and fifty years. It was filled with a thick rich pungent odour, an exquisite scent of—but (in a letter that may find its way into print) I must not say of what, for the charming old man behind the counter made us both promise that nothing should be said "in the papers" about his premises. He had an antique horror of any kind of advertisement. I hope those premises suffered no hurt in the impending war? I imagine that Tony Weller, in his day, knew them; and his son too. And this reminds me that you, James, remind me not only of St Paul's and Elia, but also of Sam Weller—though I doubt whether even *his* knowledge of London was so "extensive and peculiar" as your own.

And now, with renewed thanks to Muirhead and to you—to him for his shining mastery of spaces, to you for your glowing intimacy with corners—I am yours ever

MAX BEERBOHM

Rapallo, September 1948

Miss Dustworth and Miss Libman[1]

Y MIND has recently returned to the theme of Miss Clotilde Dustworth and Miss Mabel Libman. I don't think you know them. Before the War I used often to talk of them to Florence; but afterwards I quite forgot them. They have now—much to Florence's displeasure—recurred to me. Florence dislikes hearing about them. I myself don't exactly like *them*: I see their faults. I admit that they are both— rather dreary. But they somehow interest me. Perhaps you *do* know them? At any rate you must often have seen them both, when you have attended third or fourth performances in the playhouses. They are to be seen together in the back row of the stalls, or in the back row but one of the dress circle. They are to be seen still more often towards the *end* of the run of a play. They are pre-eminently "paper." They wear evening cloaks, with feather boas close around their throats. Underneath, they are in day clothes. Miss Dustworth (I fancy) is fifty-six years old; her friend Miss Libman not more than forty-eight. For many years—more years than I care to count—how time flies!—they have shared a very small flat on the shady side of Long Acre. They take in two papers: the *Daily Mail* and the *Era*. They were both on the stage once. Miss Dustworth indeed had a small part —a very small part—in one of the autumn dramas at "The Lane" (in the days of Gus Harris, rather than in those of Arthur Collins). Her means of subsistence are not very obvious; just what they are, and where they come from, is not known; but I have heard from her friends (who are few, and appalling) that there was "a gentleman" in the course of

1 Found among Max's papers after his death. Date unknown.

[105]

her career, and that he made a settlement. Possibly Miss Libman has a settlement, but at any rate it is less than Clotilde's. Miss Libman has the smaller of the two small rooms in Long Acre. She was a governess before she went on the boards—a governess in London. She acted only in the provinces. As actress she never got to London. She is inwardly bitter about Clotilde. But Fate has thrown these two together. They could not get on without each other. In appearance there is not much to choose between them. They both have hair of a blue-ish auburn, and are very thickly powdered. They are neither of them vain. Each of them dresses in the morning with the blind of her window pulled almost all the way down. Each powders slightly before looking in the glass. They were neither of them ever beautiful— though Miss Dustworth has been described (rightly or wrongly—wrongly, I think) as *"distinguée."* A charwoman comes in and "does for" them at noon. They are not early risers. They are fond of Guinness's stout. They don't read books very much. They never leave the four-mile radius. They used to go for a fortnight to Southsea every August, but sea air no longer agrees with them. They both, I think, have some vague internal complaint. But they are plucky, in a rather dreary way, and dismiss it from their minds. They live for the theatre. They go—for there is always an unsuccessful production *somewhere*, and there isn't a box-office keeper whom they don't know, and who doesn't know them —almost every night . . . even on nights when they have been to matinées. Indeed it is on these nights that they are least able *not* to go to a "show." Miss Dustworth has often said to Miss Libman, *"Nothing* gives me the blues so much as coming home after a Mat if one is not going somewhere in the evening." They admired greatly Waller, and were on terms of personal friendship with Mrs Waller, Florence West (of whom, in her public capacity, they always spoke as "West"). They do not know Mrs Dion Boucicault—they are far from any such knowledge. But they speak of her as Irene to their friends, and as Vanbrugh to their acquaintances. They had a very high opinion of Charles Warner's acting. About my brother Herbert they were less cordial. "Tree," Miss Dustworth would say, "is always Tree." They see talent in Gerald du Maurier, but "he's not," says Miss Libman, "a lover." Miss Dustworth always has at the theatre a small opera-glass of mother-o'-pearl, which she uses very often— though it has very bad lenses, and darkens counsel. She is always careful to hand it to Miss Libman after using it herself. Miss Libman never uses it for more than a moment or two, as being in this respect a sort of pensioner. She always hands it back with a certain suppressed bitterness. Both women had a strong feeling for King Edward. Miss Dustworth regarded him as "a sportsman." So did Miss Libman. They had a fairly strong feeling for Queen Victoria during her lifetime; but not after. Talking of death, I am reminded that they knew Mrs Crippen. They were great friends, indeed, of Mrs Crippen. For two years and more, almost every week, they used to go and have Sunday supper in Hilldrop Crescent. They used to complain to each other of the distance, but they always enjoyed themselves when they got there. They liked "the Doctor"—though it seemed to them, later, that they had never liked him, and had always seen "something wrong about that man." Their friendship with his wife was, however, to stand them in very good stead socially, after the Doctor's flight and arrest. The keeper of this and that box office had them to dinner at the Troc or the Monico on this and that Sunday night. At one time there seemed a chance that they would be sub-poena'd at the Trial. They had communicated with Scotland Yard. Inspector Drew came and visited them in Long Acre, and drank some stout with them, one summer's afternoon. Nothing, however, came of it. All the same, the period of the Crippen case was perhaps the brightest in their joint career. During the War they were very suspicious that the people in the flat above them, also those in the flat below them, were German;

also the people in the opposite flats. But they weren't asked out to dine on the strength of this. Miss Dustworth would have liked to hang the Kaiser. Miss Libman thought hanging would be too good for him. As to which of them was right, who shall decide? They think the Railwaymen need a lesson, and that the Miners are going to ruin us all, and that Iris Hoey is going to be a big actress. They don't at all care for the Cinema—partly because they are not young enough to change allegiance, partly because there is no Free-List. There is a small dark bathroom in their flat. It is here that they keep the files of the *Era*. They knew the Marquis de Leuville slightly. He once came to tea and borrowed fifteen shillings from one of them—from Miss Libman, as a matter of fact. Miss Dustworth happened to have nothing in her purse. The Marquis did not come back next day to repay the loan, though he had said he would. After the lapse of a week Miss Dustworth insisted that, as the Marquis had come to see *her*, she must make good the loss to Miss Libman. Miss Libman's pride was wounded. She said that some people never supposed any people would come for the purpose of seeing anyone but themselves. She refused the fifteen shillings. For three days neither lady spoke to the other. Such quarrels have arisen now and again. But the friendship is a lasting one, based on a genuine affinity of spirit. Perhaps I have written to you at too great length about them. I admit they are not remarkable women; not ladies exactly; narrow, uncultivated, without any fairness of vision. But am I mistaken in thinking there is a sort of awful cosiness about them? Florence thinks I am utterly mistaken in this opinion. Which of us is right? I will abide by your decision.

WORDS FOR PICTURES

"The Author of *Our Village*"
A Pen-Portrait by Maclise

"I S *THAT* MISS MITFORD?" Thus, with a little scream and with a flutter of all her ringlets, must the young lady of the period, turning the pages of Mr Maclise's album, have greeted this presentment of her favourite author. For Miss Mitford wrote in that age when a well-beloved author's face and figure were not the open secret which, thanks to camera and paragraph, they are now, but were things remote, rather, mystical and delicious, to be deduced from the manner of her books. She who wrote *Our Village* had ever been, to the entranced fancy of her public, a damsel more flower-like than any of the flowers that were so dear to her; a very Perdita, with a touch of Emily Haling, one might say, in her ethereal slimness and in "the radiant delicacy of her features —sure presage of an untimely grave." The presence that rose thus so strangely in the album was not expressive of what in the ways of a thousand editions young ladies had come to desire. Maclise had delineated Miss Mitford, not indeed without sentiment, but without fear or favour, showing her to the world as he himself had seen her in the sunny parlour of her cottage at Three-Mile Cross. And she sat there, the plump, industrious, good-humoured spinster, at a table by an open window, beyond whose honeysuckle one could see the nice landscape that inspired her. She wore a big straw bonnet over her ringlets, and a tight bertha across her bosom. There was a sheet of MS upon her lap, and a quill in her hand, and one of her sandalled feet was propped upon a hassock. Her umbrella rested against the table. "Flush," her dog, lay asleep on the carpet. And a small boy from her printer's stood near her, holding out his hand for the envelope she had just wafered. Indeed, nothing could have been more cosily prosaic than the whole portrait. But I dare say that the subject of it was not ill-pleased, and that, had she heard the shrill ejaculations of her readers, she would have revelled in their implied compliment to her work. For it was in her work that she lived really. She was one of those romantic women who must needs create for themselves the romance which nature and circumstance have denied them. It was because she was so plain that she wrote (as, in her way, she did write) so beautifully. For her, as for all women who have written well, literature was but an expedient; a means of evasion, not of expression. Rarely do beautiful women try to write. When they do, they write as ill as Lady Blessington or Mrs Norton. Given a fair face and figure, Miss Mitford would never have written two lines worth reading. But, as it was, she wrote a great many, and she was very happy in her occupation. She relished her present fame, and all the praise that friends liberally accorded to her. I dare say, too, that in her heart of hearts she thought she would get im-mortality into the bargain—does not every writer, soever modest, touchingly believe that his or her books have, at least, the subtle qualities of permanence? I like to think that somewhere in Elysium Miss Mitford's ample shade rests in the belief that she is posterity's pet. Certainly, the prime critics of her day spared no pains to assure her that her works would die only with the language they were written in. Rash prophets! her immortality has been a very short one. *Our Village*, her best work, has already gone the way of *Julian* and *Foscari*, those two tragedies which were perhaps her worst. Nobody reads her now. Maclise's portrait of her calls no shrill cry of horror from the lips of our young ladies. "And who *was* Miss Mitford?" would, I am afraid, be its utmost effect now. But really, except the consciousness of good work, present fame is the best reward that can be given to any writer. It was given, in the fullest measure, to Miss Mitford. She did her best work in Georgian days, and she reaped a rich harvest of admiration from that Early Victorian Era of which she was at once the harbinger and the incarnation. So I can hardly pretend that Miss Mitford is to be pitied. It was known that her work was preferred by the young Sovereign to that of any other writer. Till she died, in '55, she held that high charter of approval which has since passed to the bashful murderess of Delicia.

[*Saturday Review*, 30 April 1898]

"The Battle of Sant' Egidio, 1416"
A Painting by Paolo Uccello,
in the National Gallery

USK HAS FALLEN, and in a sombre cavalcade of silk and silver, under the pale banner of the Hungarians, rides Carlo Malatesta da Rimini, a captive. But such is the pride of that great warrior, and so inveterate in him the habit of command, that, even now, he points his *bâton* as though the knights behind him were all his followers, not his captors, and he were leading them to victory. The light of sure victory is in his eyes. His plump, white charger is rampant. And the profile of that curled boy, his nephew, seems to express primmest serenity, even complacency of spirit. The ground is strewn with splinters of lances, with the casques and shields that have been thrown down by *condottieri* in their flight. Among these remnants of defeat lies, mark it! the prone body of a slain knight, "terribly foreshortened." Yet Malatesta rides proudly in the pageant of upright lances, as though the notes of the Hungarian trumpets were to the tune of his own triumph. It may be that he even resents the obtrusion of that one knight who (on a white charger, plump and rampant, the very counterpart of his own) is trying so clumsily to rescue him. But for this hitch, there were nothing to mar the vesperal procession of which he is the figure-head. The dark hedge which lines the route of the procession is mooned with white roses and is all aglow with oranges and pomegranates, whilst, on the roads of the darkling hill-side beyond, what could be prettier than those men-at-arms, few and tiny, chasing one another hither and thither? What matter to Malatesta that the battle is lost, and himself a hostage? He will soon be ransomed for a sackful of ducats, and then he will rally another army for the Venetians, and Braccio da Perugia will give him his revenge. In the fifteenth century, remember, warfare was not the bitter and horrible thing it had once been and was again to be. Bravery and piety and endurance, wounds and death, were not essential to it. It was the first medium through which the spirit of the Renaissance sought expression, and victory lay with whichever army was, in ordering and equipage, the more beautiful. The first care of a commander in those days was for the breed of his soldiers' horses, for the fashion and sheen of panoplies, for the harmonious coxcombry of plumes and crests. His second, and perhaps his greater, care was for nice symmetry in the disposition of his legions upon the field. Any blows which might be desultorily exchanged with the enemy were a mere survival, a dramatic pretence, in no way pertinent to the issue. The artistic sensibility of the age was such that no commander could persuade his men to stand against an enemy which had obviously outdone them in beauty. And it was according to this code that all European battles were fought both by sea and by land, until Sir Francis Drake, taking advantage of his own Philistinism, insulted with petty violence that great crescent of superbly painted and gilded galleons which swept through the English waters, "wonderful great and strong" even to him. When storm destroyed all that Drake had left of the Armada, it was felt that aesthetic warfare was doomed, and another era of warfare on the basis of bravery was initiated forthwith—an era which has been ended only recently by the inventions of science. But, even as Messrs Whitehead, Maxim and the rest have not put all personal conflict quite outside the range of possibility, so, in the days of the Renaissance, did it sometimes happen that a few soldiers really wounded one another. In this picture of Uccello's, the scattered fragments of weapons seem to point to a probability that the two armies had been rather equally matched in beauty, and that a certain amount of doubt and personal irritation had thus crept into the conflict. But note that not one orange has fallen from the hedge, not one plume has been deranged, nor crest crumpled, and that the great red turban which swathes the brow of Malatesta himself is a very triumph of neatness! It is probable that those fragments were merely sprinkled along the route for mere purposes of dramatic effect. I suspect there is no one really in the prone suit of armour above which the plump and dark-green horse of that Hungarian knight is so exceptionally rampant.

[*Saturday Review*, 30 April 1898]

" 'Musidora' Bathing Her Feet"
A Painting by Thomas Gainsborough

T IS ORDAINED that he who enters in at Art's sacred temple, near the lions and fountains, must leave behind him, as a Western equivalent for slippers, his umbrella. And what is an Englishman without his umbrella? Take it from him, and you rob him of the staff he leans on through Life's pilgrimage. It is the Excalibur he brandishes in all battles—disarm him of it, and he is your prisoner. It is his crozier, sceptre, fairy-wand. It is the very plinth and emblem of all his majesty, and his soul is in its folds. Beer and the Bible, according to his neighbours, are the explanation of him; but we who know him well know well that he depends on neither of these wholesome stimulants. It is the umbrella which has made Englishmen what they are, and its material is the stuff of which Englishmen are made. Now, strong in these Englishmen is their aversion from fine art—their indignation at the sight of it. Send them umbrelliferous into a gallery of fine pictures, and the place would be wrecked in less than no time. I do not so much mean that they would, in their wrath, scrape and perforate the canvases with the ferules of their umbrellas—though that is probably how they would proceed —as that the very tenure of their umbrellas would make them bold to express themselves with that practicalness for which they are so famous. And so I think that it is a wise ordinance which makes the Englishman here surrender his umbrella for a disc of metal. It saves, not only the pictures from laceration, but also the gallery from being over-crowded. Many Englishmen flatly refuse to go whither their

umbrellas may not go. Few can bear to be parted from them
for more than a quarter of an hour, or at most twenty
minutes. Their arms hang limply, their fingers soon begin
to twitch convulsively for the familiar handle, and the longing to redeem their pledge draws them back irresistibly to
the turnstiles, out into the Square. True, the average man,
as he wanders by the pictures, can caress the disc in his
waistcoat pocket, somewhat lulling himself with the knowledge that it is a hostage for his umbrella; but the harsh fact
remains that it is *not* an umbrella, and he is ill at ease. He is but
a humbled, dispirited, almost denationalised creature, a shell
or shadow of his true self. He has no capacity for protest; he
is susceptible to any influence. Even to the influence of
Beauty must he succumb here. Figure to yourself how, given
his umbrella, he would rage at the sight of that picture
which confronts him at the very outset, that faint and lovely
picture, Gainsborough's "Musidora"! What, I have sometimes wondered, is the oval of that one gilt frame that it
should bound so much incomparable beauty? Surely there is
nothing in the whole world to match that nude figure, fair
and slim as a narcissus, so listless in the dense shadow of the
trees, yet so alert with health in every curve of it. "She has
been yonder, running in the hot light of the noon," one
guesses. "She is too young to be tired with her exertions;
but now that she finds herself in the shade here, sitting with
one foot in the cold, clear, dark waters of a brook, she has
surrendered herself, insensibly, to the still magic of this
place and moment." Yes! One of her feet is among the rushes
in the running water; the other is crossed upon her knee,
and she, drooping forward with eyes downcast, slowly un-
binds the sandal from it. A strand of her red-gold hair has
slipped its tire and lies over her shoulder. Her waist and
arms are caught in a film of drapery. There is no expression,
save that of flawless beauty, in her profile. Musidora? That
tawdry figurine in Thomson's confectionery? Likelier, this
is some great lady of the day of Gainsborough, some reigning

beauty of St James's, who is but foolishly pretending to be Musidora. Surely, some delicate patrician, whose profile, seen for a passing moment at the window of her emblazoned and many-lackeyed coach, may have often thrilled our great-grandfathers in the Mall, even as here it thrills us. Those ladies who, for their own whim or their painter's, pretended to be some one else, always betrayed themselves. Think of Lady Spencer as "Queen of the Harem" in Léotard's pastel: despite the veil and the ottoman, is she not an English gentlewoman to her finger-tips, which she has so conscientiously stained with saffron? And the Duchess of Queensberry, though she had grey eyes—what could be less like Minerva than she according to Sir Joshua? Equally weak at impersonation were all the other great ladies, except Lady Hamilton who, poor soul! was actress by nature and great lady in name only. Indeed, they could not impersonate at all—they merely dressed up. And dressing-up was a charming foible. I wish it were still in vogue. But stay! Dressing-up is one thing: undressing-up is another. Nor can one suppose that these great ladies ever undressed-up as any one but themselves. My theory of this picture must be wrong. I wonder now that I could ever have imagined this figure to be artificially posed. Its freedom and listless grace could belong only to some archaic darling of the woods and the hills and the rushing waters. Musidora? No, not Musidora!—would that misnomer had not saved that pseudo-classic minx from the oblivion she deserved! . . . Diana? Yes, I believe this figure to be Diana herself, resting from the chase, and this green sanctuary of hers to be somewhere at the foot of Erymanthus. I must not stay, lest she turn her head suddenly and see me, another Actaeon, spying on her. You know what became of Actaeon! I must move away quickly. Were I to reappear at the turnstile with a pair of antlers to my brow, they might refuse to give me back my umbrella. And to me, who am a free-born Englishman (more or less), that seems too terrible a contingency!   [*Saturday Review*, 13 August 1898]

"Punting" A Drawing
by Rex Whistler

ERY EVOCATIVE, yes, this little picture; particularly so, poignantly so, to one who has beheld with the eyes of boyhood the very things Rex Whistler has but reconstructed from hearsay and from documents. *Tout passe, toute casse, tout lasse.* "Changing London." *Hélas!* The March of Time. *Vixere fortes. Eheu fugaces.* All, all are gone, the old familiar faces. *Et ego in Arcadia.*

Very Arcadian, yes, Hyde Park still was when the Serpentine flowed up within a few feet of the Marble Arch, reflecting on its way the sallow and rounded northern houses of Park Lane—the house that was once Mrs Fitzherbert's, and all those others. I cannot say that I much liked the Quadriga that had been put upon the Arch to commemorate the Shah of Persia's visit in 1873. It was (I still think) one of Boehm's least good works. But I was rather furious when it was removed by a short Act of Parliament in 1881. And I was mad with rage when, some nine years later, I saw demolished the dear old moss-grown Rockery, a structure of uncertain origin, but redolent of the mermaid who had from time immemorial, and till so recently, swum around and about it.

While she lived, one had taken her as a matter of course. She was just one of the normal anomalies of our town, like the two milkmaids in St James's Park, or the Piccadilly goat; and, like them, she was very decorous—except on the one occasion which Rex Whistler has recorded. Heaven only knows what she saw in Mr Spingham. She cannot have liked his blazer or his pince-nez or his black kid gloves. I knew him and Mrs Spingham slightly (*very* slightly, I am glad to say) and am the man whom you see in the distance bowing to them from a hansom at the moment of the mermaid's sudden rising from the water. I heard Mrs Spingham's scream; I saw her loss of balance, her immersion, and her gallant rescue by the mermaid. I supposed she would be grateful, be forgiving. But she was hardly dry before she began writing violent letters to the Press. Questions were asked in the House of Commons. The Ranger of Parks bowed under the storm, and by his order the mermaid was shot. I shall always maintain that this was murder.

[*The New Forget-Me-Not*, 1929]

"Suppose——"A Drawing
by Rex Whistler

"YOUR OLD MEN," said one of the minor but not least truthful prophets, "shall dream dreams, your young men shall see visions." Rex Whistler is young, and therefore such a house as Blanwick Hall, built by Robert Adam for the third Marquess of Cloby, raises for him a great clear vision, and for me nothing but a humdrum dream.

I dream of the time when there was nothing absurd about so great a Hall, as home for a few people no bigger than we are; when even the baby at the Marchioness' breast would have puled in protest had there been less vast a space between it and the ceiling and the walls; when the breast of the Marquess had always a star or two on it even at breakfast; when Charles Fox was a frequent guest, and Mr Burke was invited once or twice; when William Lamb, later, spent here the first days of his honeymoon with Lady Caroline; when Luttrell jested here, and Greville grunted, and Moore warbled, and Lady Holland made herself thoroughly disagreeable, and Macaulay couldn't stop talking. Halcyon days! And days not utterly unlike them continued even into our present century.

Youth is violent. Youth is un-English. Youth reads without horror the history of foreign nations, and such things as the burning of the Châteaux do not appal it, whereas it is slightly irritated by the tame conclusions to such things as the Gordon Riots, the unrest of 1830, the Luddite and the Chartist uprisings, the Railway Strike of 1919, the General Strike of 1926. All these threats *might* have led straight to a peripety. Suppose———! That is what Rex Whistler has been doing: fondly supposing. I am not sure of the exact moment he has hit on. The bicycle hardly assorts with the nurse's crinoline. But the spirit that informs the whole supposition is unmistakable. I mark the fine sweep and swing of the embannered onrush, all unified by the idealism of the insurgents. I take note that all the members of the hitherto governing class are ungracefully fleeing in craven panic—all except the old Marquess, who is disabled by gout. Ah, cruel young Whistler, mightn't *some* of them have not disgraced their breed?

Well, they weren't put to the test. Blanwick never was invaded and burnt. That isn't the English way. Blanwick, with the Muses and the Graces along its coping, and the Virtues and the Victories, stands where Blanwick stood. One sees it now and again on the back page of *The Times*. Some day it will be a local museum, or a lunatic asylum, or an ambitious boarding-school, or just a ruin.

[*The New Keepsake*, 1931]

"Ten Years Ago . . ."[1]

EN YEARS AGO, on the edge of the world, a rather unsuccessful jerry-builder erected a small house. He built it with his own hands, and without consulting an architect, relying wholly on his own taste, which was bad, and on his own sense of measurement, which was even worse. But his commercial instinct was keen enough for him to realise that the house was unlettable. He cut his losses and went away.

Now it so happened that at that time a young man, named Edgar Smithson, who was a clerk in a provincial and rather unsuccessful bank, misappropriated a small sum of money, with which he purchased a suit from a branch of the firm of Mallaby Deely. He did not look well in the suit, for his legs were very badly formed. Also, his theft was quickly detected and he was discharged, but not prosecuted. He walked in deep dejection to the edge of the world, and saw there the vacant house. "At any rate," he muttered, "I can have a roof to my head." He was wrong. He could not enter the house, though he was rather below the middle height. The house was not tall enough for habitation. So he stood outside, staring down in deep dejection.

Now it so happened a few days later that to that edge of the world there came another discharged and malformed clerk. Neither of the two liked the look of the other. No words passed between them. The first-comer did not move. The new-comer passed by him and stood looking, for want of

[1] The picture reproduced opposite (artist unknown) was hanging in the Abinger cottage in which Sydney and Violet Schiff housed Max and his wife for most of the Second World War. Max was fascinated by it, and eventually wrote this explanation, which, without word said, he pasted on to the back of the frame, where much later it was discovered.

anything better to do, out across the edge of the world.

They were not long alone together. For it so happened that a malformed boy, who had recently escaped from Borstal, found his way to the spot where Smithson and the other man (who had no name at all) were standing. He liked the looks of neither of them and sat dully down beneath one of the two plane-trees which were the only pleasant feature of the scene.

And on the following day it so happened that the scene became more populous, though perhaps not much more pleasant. Two females wandered into it. One was a discharged cook, of whom long ago, before she grew very stout, some short-sighted person had said that she looked rather like a Madonna. The other woman had not been discharged from any post, for she had never occupied one, had never been qualified for one. The fact that she had nothing to commend or discommend her but a Grecian profile, and a tin apron that was much too long for her, had prejudiced employers against her. She had never had anything to do. She felt it was time to do something now. She stationed herself on one side of Smithson. On his other side the discharged cook did likewise. They did not look at him, for they felt they had nothing in common with him. They did not look at each other, for the same reason. Yet these two had, though they refused to recognise it, one point in common. They were both of them instable. The ex-cook was always tumbling over sideways. The woman with the Grecian profile was for ever falling down on her back.

They were not happy, these five persons outside the uninhabitable little new house. They often yearned to throw themselves over the edge of the world and explore infinity. But they lacked initiative. They had little will power. They are still standing where they stood. And from time to time Mr —— comes to them and says to them brightly "You make a pattern."

[125]